LATIN AMERICA SERIES

Series Editors,
Samuel L. Baily and Ronald T. Hyman

Samuel L. Baily and Ronald T. Hyman (Editors): *Perspectives on Latin America*

Franklin W. Knight: *The African Dimension in Latin American Societies*

Robert J. Alexander: *Agrarian Reform in Latin America*

Douglas Chalmers: *Social Change, Politics and Revolution in Latin America*

Frank Dauster: *Literature and Contemporary Latin American Affairs*

Warren Dean: *Latin America: The Struggle to End Poverty*

Agrarian Reform
in Latin America

The photographs in this book were taken by
Samuel L. Baily.

Copyright © 1974 by Robert J. Alexander

All rights reserved. No part of this book may be reproduced or transmitted in any form or by any means, electronic or mechanical, including photocopying, recording or by any information storage and retrieval system, without permission in writing from the Publisher.

Macmillan Publishing Co., Inc.
866 Third Avenue, New York, N.Y. 10022
Collier-Macmillan Canada Ltd.

Library of Congress Cataloging in Publication Data

Alexander, Robert Jackson, date
    Agrarian reform in Latin America. *see slip*

  (Latin America series)
    1. Land reform—Latin America. I. Title.
HD320.5.Z63A44   333.3'23'098   73-11733
ISBN 0-02-500770-X

First Printing 1974

Printed in the United States of America

Agrarian Reform in Latin America

Robert J. Alexander

MACMILLAN PUBLISHING CO., INC.
New York

COLLIER MACMILLAN PUBLISHERS
London

Macmillan Publishing Co., Inc.
866 Third Avenue, New York, N.Y. 10022
Collier-Macmillan Canada Ltd.

Library of Congress Cataloging in Publication Data

Alexander, Robert Jackson, date 1918–
    Agrarian reform in Latin America. *see slip*

  (Latin America series)
    1. Land reform—Latin America. I. Title.
HD320.5.Z63A44   333.3'23'098   73-11733
ISBN 0-02-500770-X

First Printing 1974
Printed in the United States of America

TO MAX GIDEONSE

Contents

Preface to the Series

THIS SERIES OF books on Latin America grew out of a summer institute we directed at Rutgers University in 1967. The institute was sponsored by Rutgers University and supported financially by the National Defense Education Act (NDEA). We invited forty-five teachers from all over the United States to live on our campus for six weeks, to study Latin American issues, and to design with us ways of teaching these issues to their students. We also brought in leading scholars and journalists with special knowledge of Latin America to help us in our work.

These books reflect what we learned from our institute experience. The task of translating our ideas into a series of books, however, has not ben easy. Two general problems have confronted us and it is well to recognize them here since their solutions have become the backbone of all of these books. First, there is the question arising from history and the social sciences: how can a person from one country or one culture adequately understand the issues facing a person from another country or another culture? The major obstacle in the path of the North American student who wishes to understand Latin America is his cultural bias. What he will learn about Latin America depends to a considerable extent upon his point of view, or his frame of reference. People see what their frame of reference prepares them to see, and most North Americans are simply not prepared to see Latin America as Latin Americans do.

A person's cultural bias or frame of reference is determined by many things including nationality, social class, religion, economic class, historical heritage, education, and technological skills. Can we in the United States—members of a highly industrialized, predominantly Protestant, democratic society—understand the people of the developing, Catholic, and for the most part authoritarian societies of Latin America? Can we whose revolution is part of the distant past sympathize with the Mexicans, Bolivians, and Cubans whose revolutions are part of the present? Is it possible for middle class, North American students to understand the life of the inhabitants of the shanty towns surrounding modern cities like Buenos Aires, Rio de Janeiro, Lima, and Santiago? Can we see the world as a variety of Latin Americans see it?

There is no simple answer to these questions. Though we may never be able to remove our own particular cultural bias, we can and must adjust our frame of reference so that we will be able to understand Latin Americans and the issues facing them. If we recognize that we have a cultural bias which determines what we see and we compare our bias with that of the people we are studying, we will have a good chance of understanding what others think and feel.

The second question concerns education: how can we meaningfully teach a person something about the issues facing people in another country? Here again there is no simple answer. We do know, however, that a person will read—and understand what he reads—when the topic is of interest to him and related to his own experience. Furthermore, we believe a reader prefers to examine these topics which call upon him to participate in the search for answers. He is not satisfied with simple, pat answers for he knows from his own experience that life is complex. Important issues are interrelated and cut across geographical areas and academic disciplines. A person is willing to participate in the search for answers, even though this approach requires a great expenditure of mental and physical effort, because this approach is meaningful and rewarding to him.

We are convinced that people will understand more about Latin America by analyzing a few key issues in depth than by attempting to learn the names of kings, viceroys, military heroes, presidents, capital cities, mountain ranges, rivers, and so forth that so often fill the pages of textbooks. We are also convinced that readers prefer—and will benefit significantly from—the study of the conflict and tension of man's affairs since these things are an important part of reality.

In summary, the books in this series will:

1. Focus on important issues rather than on a chronological coverage of Latin America.

2. Relate Latin American issues to similar issues in the United States.

3. Emphasize differing points of view to help the reader clarify his own frame of reference.

4. Emphasize controversy as a meaningful approach to the teaching of social studies.

5. Permit and encourage the reader to work with the "stuff" of Latin American studies by presenting relevant documents, maps, charts, and photographs.

6. Focus on the questions of when and how we can legitimately formulate generalizations about Latin America, whether or not we can speak of Latin America as a whole, and whether it is the similarities or the differences among the Latin American countries that are more important.

7. Discuss issues which are representative of those facing other sections of the world besides the Western Hemisphere.

The intent of the editors and authors is to present Latin America to the reader in an open-ended way. We recognize that these books can not encompass all of the important information and interpretations about the area. Our purpose is to provide a basis from which the reader can further his understanding of Latin America today.

New Brunswick, New Jersey
September, 1973

—SAMUEL L. BAILY
RONALD T. HYMAN

Editors' Introduction

It is obvious to everyone who is even slightly familiar with contemporary Latin America that agrarian reform is an important issue. It has been one of the most important components of the Mexican, Bolivian, and Cuban Revolutions; the governments of other Latin American countries have carried out agrarian reform in various degrees, and agrarian reform is a major aspiration of most peasants in the countries which have not yet attempted it.

We in the United States who are unfamiliar with agrarian reform in our time, usually find it difficult to realize how pressing this issue is for others. Nevertheless, in the past we had an agrarian reform and it is for this reason that Professor Alexander begins his book with a quote describing the confiscation of Tory land in New England during the American Revolution. Hopefully this awareness of our own past will better enable us to understand agrarian reform in Latin America today.

Robert J. Alexander, professor of Economics at Rutgers University and author of more than a dozen books on various subjects concerning contemporary Latin America, focuses primarily on agrarian reform in Mexico, Bolivia, Venezuela, and Cuba. Using these four as models, he explores such issues as the purposes for which agrarian reform is carried out, how the land is taken, if or how the land is paid for, who gets the land, and what kind of educational and financial support accompany the agrarian reform. Professor Alexander also compares the similarities and differences of the agrarian reform programs in these four countries.

Following is a list of questions which we feel would be useful to keep in mind when reading the book:
1. What are the basic common characteristics of all four of the agrarian reforms discussed?

2. What are the distinguishing characteristics of each?

3. In which ways have Bolivia, Venezuela, and Cuba patterned their reforms after that of Mexico?

4. In light of the knowledge gained by studying the agrarian reforms of Mexico, Bolivia, Venezuela, and Cuba, is it possible to predict whether future agrarian reforms will come about by peaceful means or only through violent upheaval?

5. Does Professor Alexander sympathize with the agrarian reforms of one country more than those in the other countries? How do you know? If he does, in what ways does his preference influence his treatment of the other reforms?

6. How do you measure the success of an agrarian reform program? What are the major economic, political, and social results of agrarian reform in Mexico, Bolivia, Venezuela, and Cuba? Which kinds of results are most important?

7. What should the attitude of the United States government be toward any future agrarian reform program in Latin America? Is agrarian reform in Latin America in the best interest of the United States? If it is, is our government doing everything it can to promote it?

In addition, we believe it would be valuable to compare Professor Alexander's analysis of agrarian reform in Latin America with the analyses presented in other books in this series. Two books in particular are most germane: Warren Dean, *Latin America: The Struggle to End Poverty,* and Samuel L. Baily and Ronald T. Hyman (eds.), *Perspectives on Latin America.*

—S. L. B.
R. T. H.

Author's Preface

FOR SOME YEARS, the issue of agrarian reform has been a major one in Latin America. However, there has been little attempt to take an overall view of its extent and significance in Latin America. The present volume is a modest attempt to do this.

The writing of this book was undertaken after an invitation from my colleagues Professor Samuel Baily of the History Department of Rutgers University and Professor Ronald Hyman of the Rutgers Graduate School of Education. They sought the volume as a contribution to a series of books dealing with key issues in contemporary Latin American society.

I was happy to accept this invitation for two reasons. First of all, there is no question concerning the relevance of agrarian reform in the nations lying south of the United States. In addition, the subject has engaged my interest for many years. Although I have written several articles on it, I had never had the opportunity to write a full book on it.

As always, the author owes many debts to people who have contributed to the elaboration of his subject. First, there are Professors Baily and Hyman, whom I must thank both for the opportunity to write this book in the first place, and for their meticulous editorial work on the manuscript. Then, there are numerous people in Latin America who responded to my requests for details concerning agrarian reform in their particular countries. I shall not begin to mention their names, for fear that I may inadvertently leave out someone among them who should have been included.

Finally, I must mention my wife, Joan, and my children, Tony and Meg, who as always, have listened to me talk endlessly about Latin American agrarian reform when they would have preferred to talk about something else, and who have borne with my tapping on the typewriter while I should have been talking or playing with them.

Rutgers University   —ROBERT J. ALEXANDER
June, 1973

Agrarian Reform
in Latin America

Introduction

. . . . great confiscations of Tory estates were carried out by the state legislatures, generally in the height of the war. New Hampshire confiscated twenty-eight estates, including the large property of its governor, Sir John Wentworth. In Massachusetts a sweeping act confiscated at one blow all the property of all who had fought against the United States or had even retired into places under British authority without permission from the American government. Among the lands confiscated by special mention were those of Sir William Pepperell, the second baronet of that name, whose vast estate in Maine extended so far along the coast that it was said he could ride all the way from Kittery Point to Saco, a distance of thirty miles, on his own land. In New York, all lands and rents of the crown and all estates of fifty-nine named persons were confiscated, the greatest among them, probably being that of the Philipse connection. Probably something like three hundred square miles of the old Philipse estate were confiscated, bringing value of several hundred thousand dollars. By 1782 the state of New York had confiscated royal property in land valued at $2,500,000 in hard money. In all, the state probably received $3,150,000 Spanish dollars for forfeited real estate. . . . Altogether it is evident that a great deal of land changed hands, and that the confiscation of Tory estates contributed powerfully to break up the system of large landed properties, since the state usually sold the lands thus acquired in much smaller parcels. . . .*

THIS QUOTATION describes agrarian reform in the United States during the American Revolution. In essence, the changes here were like agrarian reform anywhere else: land belonging to one group of people was taken away and transferred to another group. As in Latin America, agrarian reform in the United States took place in an atmosphere of revolutionary change and it profoundly altered the society and economy of the states in which it was carried out. It also provoked some of the same questions. Should large landholdings be divided into small family farms? Should those whose land is seized be compensated for their losses? Should those who receive land under agrarian reform have to pay for it?

In Latin America, agrarian reform has been carried out in several countries during the present century. And in all twenty re-

*Jameson, *The American Revolution Considered as a Social Movement* (Princeton N.J.: Princeton University Press, 1940), p. 34.

1

publics the issue of agrarian reform has grown in importance during recent decades. Whether the large landholdings which predominate in most of these countries should be broken up and redistributed is, in fact, one of the most bitterly contested of political issues. Several countries have adopted large-scale land redistribution programs, and these have had wide effects on their economies, social structures, cultural life, and politics. Other countries have undertaken less ambitious land reform programs. Through the Alliance for Progress, agrarian reform is an objective that all Latin American nations are pledged to fulfill, sooner or later.

It is this changing pattern of land ownership in Latin America that is the subject of this book. Before we look at the process in detail, it is necessary to define some of the terms we shall be using, note some of the principal issues involved in the change, and place the whole question in historical perspective.

WHAT IS AGRARIAN REFORM?

Right at the outset it is essential to define just what is meant by "agrarian reform." The key element is the change in land ownership, the transfer of possession of land from one group in the society to another.

Agrarian reform must be distinguished from "agricultural reform." This involves changes in the way land is used, advances in the technology applied to it, new ways of transporting the products to market, and changes in many other aspects of the work and life of the farmer.

As we shall show later, if agrarian reform is to be economically successful, it must be accompanied by agricultural reform. Land redistribution alone cannot increase production and improve the material well-being of the new landholders. They need various forms of assistance, including credit, instruction in better farming, improved strains of seed, advice about possible markets for their products, and help in getting the products to market.

It should be clear that one *can* have agrarian reform without agricultural reform, just as one *can* have agricultural reform without redistributing the land. Our attention, however, will be concentrated on the problems posed by the change in land ownership in Latin America. Changes in land use and technology will be treated only as they relate to land redistribution.

WHAT ARE THE PRINCIPAL ISSUES IN AGRARIAN REFORM?

In the pages that follow, the reader will find frequent reference to certain issues surrounding the basic problem of redistributing the land in Latin America. It is well to note here what the most important of these issues are.

First, there are the objectives of agrarian reform—the purposes for which land redistribution is carried out. These purposes are economic, social, and political.

Economically, land redistribution is undertaken because governments believe that the existing pattern of ownership hampers the expansion and modernization of agriculture. It is hoped that by taking the land away from those with little incentive to improve it or increase output, and transferring it to others with more incentive, both output and productivity will improve.

Agrarian reform is also carried out as one way of correcting social inequalities in the various Latin American countries. Under the traditional system, the owners generally treat those who work on the land as servants or even slaves. The system has kept the tenants, sharecroppers, and agricultural laborers illiterate, and afforded them completely inadequate medical and other services. Land redistribution is undertaken as a first step toward bringing about more equitable social conditions in the countryside.

Finally, the traditional landlords are widely accused of using their powerful political influence to hold back economic development and to perpetuate social inequality. From a political point of view, agrarian reform is therefore a process which, in taking away the land of the large landowners, destroys the economic foundation upon which their political power is based.

A second major category of issues that will be raised in this book concerns the way in which agrarian reform is brought about. On this depends, at least in part, the extent to which the reform's objectives are fulfilled. Several questions are crucial here. Did agrarian reform take place through violence and during social upheaval or, instead, through a more or less orderly and democratic process? Did the landlords keep any land, or did they lose it all? Were they compensated for their former lands? Finally, to whom did the land go? Was it turned over to individual peasant families? Was it granted to peasant cooperatives? Or did it pass to the State, which took the place of the former private landowners?

All of these issues will be discussed in the chapters which follow. Finally, we shall investigate the actual results of agrarian reform in those countries where it has been widely applied. We shall note its economic, social, and political impact.

DEFINITIONS

A number of terms used in this book might not be familiar to the reader and we shall define the most important.

First, we may note the phrases used throughout this volume that are synonymous with "agrarian reform." Whenever we use "land reform" or "land redistribution program," we shall mean the same as "agrarian reform."

One important distinction must be made between "confiscation" and "expropriation." In the former, property is seized without its owners receiving any compensation whatsoever. In the latter, those who lose their property are compensated, at least in part.

Important, too, in the pages that follow will be the terms *latifundia* and *minifundia*. Much of Latin American agriculture is characterized by these two opposite types of landholding: the very large estates and the very small holdings, too small to provide their owners with an adequate living. The very large holdings are known generally in Latin America as *latifundios*, and the small holdings as *minifundios*.

We shall be talking a great deal about large landed properties, and since the names sometimes differ from country to country, we shall have to vary our nomenclature accordingly. Thus, the words *haciendas*, or *estancias*, or *fundos* (this word used particularly in Chile), all mean very extensive property holdings.

Finally, we shall use the word "plantation" to refer to a large landed estate which is cultivated by modern methods, with the use of considerable capital equipment, usually by workers who are paid wages, and usually producing a single product such as sugar, cotton, or bananas, largely for sale abroad. The plantation is quite different from most other large landholdings in Latin America, which usually employ more primitive methods and are worked by peasants who rent parts of the property, paying their rent either in money (which is exceptional), by sharing part of their crop with the owner of the land, or by rendering him some kind of personal service. Peasants who pay their rent with a share of their crop are usually referred to in English as "sharecroppers."

HISTORICAL PRECEDENTS

Agrarian reform is an old idea in human history. Many civilizations have regarded concentration of land in a few hands as harmful and set about redistributing the land. In the Palestine of early biblical times, land was redistributed periodically during the Year of Jubilee, which fell every fifty years. The purpose was to break up the large landholdings and assure that each farming family had enough land to meet it needs.

Likewise, in ancient Greece, a number of the city-states instituted agrarian reforms. One of the most famous was the extensive redistribution of land carried out by Solon in Athens at the beginning of the sixth century B.C.

During the eight-hundred-year history of the Roman Republic and Empire, redistribution of land was frequent. Both Tiberius and Gaius Gracchus were famous reformers who broke up many of the large estates which by the second century B.C. dominated much of the Italian peninsula. Julius Caesar and many of the emperors who succeeded him carried out similar redistributions in various parts of the empire, particularly to settle veterans of the Roman legions on land of their own.

From the sixteenth to the eighteenth centuries in England, extensive redistribution took place but of quite a different kind. In this case, private landlords were authorized to take over and fence in "common lands" which since the Middle Ages had been open to the use of all residents of a manor or village for the grazing of their animals and for provision of firewood and construction materials. This was the famous Enclosure Movement, which started at least as early as the reign of Queen Elizabeth I and did not come to an end until the reign of George III.

One of the most famous and widespread agrarian reforms of modern times took place in France during the French Revolution in the 1790's. At that time, the lands belonging to the nobility, the Crown, and the Church were seized and turned over to the former tenants. This brought into existence the landowning peasant class which has been the backbone of the French economy and political life for almost two hundred years.

During the twentieth century, agrarian reforms have been carried out in many countries of the Old World, under a wide variety of political and economic regimes. One of the earliest was in Russia in 1917, when the Bolsheviks, in one of their first acts after seizing power, nationalized all land but gave the peasants the right to occupy and work their landlords' former holdings. A decade later, the government of Stalin decreed a second agrarian reform, taking away the land from the peasants in turn and forcing them into "collective" or "state" farms, both under close governmental control.

After World War II, other Communist governments also carried out agrarian reforms on the Soviet model, first granting the land to the peasants, and later forcing the small landowners into collective and state farms. This was the pattern in Eastern Europe, as well as the Communist-controlled countries of Asia. However, in the 1950's the Communist governments of Poland and Yugoslavia permitted the peasants once again to run their own farms, and both of these countries are today characterized by family farms.

Agrarian reform in Europe, Africa, and Asia has by no means been limited to Communist regimes. After World War I, the kingdom of Rumania redistributed most of the large estates among the former tenants. For more than twenty years since World War II the Christian Democrat governments of Italy have been carrying out a land redistribution program in the southern part of the country. In Egypt, the revolutionary government of Gamal Abdel Nasser carried through an extensive agrarian reform in the 1950's; and in the late 1950's the Shah of Iran first distributed all of his own lands to the peasants on them, and then enacted a general law breaking up all large private estates and turning the land over to the peasants.

After World War II, the American occupation forces in Japan and South Korea, under the command of General Douglas Mac-Arthur, imposed a thoroughgoing agrarian reform on both countries, turning over the large estates to small peasant proprietors. A more modest agrarian reform was also undertaken with United States encouragement in South Vietnam. India, Burma, Algeria, and Kenya are some of the other countries which have adopted large land redistribution programs during the post–World War II period.

In America, too, agrarian reform has a long history. During the Inca Empire, which at the arrival of the Spaniards included part or all of the modern South American republics of Peru, Colombia, Ecuador, Bolivia, Argentina, and Chile, land redistribution took place periodically. The agricultural land of each village was redistributed among the heads of families living in the village. The land allotted to each family was increased or reduced to correspond with changes in the size of the family since the last redistribution.

As noted earlier, the United States experienced agrarian reform during the American Revolution. About fifty years later, more large-scale seizures took place in southern New York State and large estates were divided among the farmers who had been tenants.

Finally, in the wake of the Civil War, the proposal was made by Senator Charles Sumner and other Radical Republican leaders, that agrarian reform be carried out in the ex-Confederate states. This proposal, which became famous under the slogan "forty acres and a mule," urged the federal government to seize the land of large estate-owners who had supported the Confederacy, and divide it among the former Negro slaves and white farmers with little or no land. Although small efforts along these lines were made in a few Southern states, the Sumner program was not generally adopted by the national government.

CONCLUSION

The basic element of agrarian reform is the transfer of land from one group to another, and this has happened repeatedly in human history. Many ancient civilizations carried out redistributions of land. In modern times, people of the most diverse political tendencies have supported it, and the United States itself has experienced agrarian reform, both within its borders and in other countries temporarily under its control. As we turn to the problem in Latin America, it should thus be clear that land redistribution has been world-wide in application and is not the monopoly of any one political group.

There are many facets to the apparently simple problem of transferring landed property from one group to another in Latin American society. There are many ways in which this can be carried out, and the results of agrarian reform can differ widely. In the following chapters, we shall consider in some detail some of the complications posed by agrarian reform.

1 / The Question of Agrarian Reform in Latin America

The plantation with its *patron* and *peones*, with the *capataz* (foreman) between, the *capataz*—who remained a Spaniard even if the *patron* was a Mexican—with the *capataz* on the place, even if the *patron* lived in Paris—riding a spirited horse, a pistol at his belt, a whip in his hand, acting as administrator, as judge, as mighty lord over a peon population which was tied to the soil by debts it could not pay, by the tradition of slavery, by affection for the only home it knew—this plantation resting upon force . . . has been the dominant feature of the Mexican scene. . . .

The plantation was Mexico. It paid few taxes. It built no roads. It imported nothing from the outside, and exported next-to-nothing. It made no effort to improve the tillage, the tools, the crops or the lives of its dependents. . . . It was not a business enterprise that had been built up by purchase and capital saving, it was the fruit of the Conquest, the result of theft, robbery and murder, of age-long conflict with the neighboring villages. It was . . . a dead weight upon the economic life of the country. It lived on rentals, by indirect tillage, by leaving the risk of planting to be borne by the peon. . . .*

THIS VIVID DESCRIPTION of a prerevolutionary Mexican *hacienda* by the late Professor Frank Tannenbaum might, with some modification of detail, have applied until recent years to most rural areas of Latin America. The large landholding of the region (the *hacienda*, or *fundo*, or *estancia* in Spanish-speaking countries and the *fazenda* in Portuguese-speaking Brazil) has been the place where the majority of the people of Latin America lived.

As the quotation points out, the traditional large landholdings of Latin America did not owe their origins to economic forces. They did not develop from small farms which grew into larger ones with the use of capital equipment and more modern techniques. Rather, they originated with the Spanish and Portuguese conquerors who seized the land from the Indians and then divided

---

*Frank Tannenbaum, *Peace by Revolution* (New York: Columbia University Press, 1933), p. 188.

it—and the Indians—among themselves. To understand what happened, we must look quickly at the historical evolution of the large landholding system in Latin America.

ORIGINS OF LARGE LANDHOLDINGS

The large landholding system in Latin America had its origins in the conquest of Latin America by the Spaniards and Portuguese in the sixteenth century. The conquerors (or *conquistadores* in Spanish and Portuguese) established institutions to assure their continued control over the lands they seized and the people living on them. In doing so, they adapted to new uses institutions with which they were familiar in the Old World.

In the Spanish areas, two such institutions were of particular importance: the *encomienda* and the *mita*. Both originated in medieval Spain.

During the seven hundred years before Columbus "discovered" the New World, the Christian Spaniards waged an intermittent crusade against the Moslem Moors, who had conquered most of the Iberian Peninsula in the eighth century. As the Christian kingdoms of the peninsula regained territory from the Moors, the Christian nobles were granted control over both the people in the reconquered areas and the land on which they lived. The nobles were charged with the duties of seeing that the Moslems were converted to Christianity and rendering military service to the king whenever called for. In return, the nobles received tribute in goods and money from the people under their control and "protection." This system was known as the *encomienda*.

Medieval Spain also was characterized by the phenomenon of communal labor—work done in common by the peasants generally for the benefit of the community as a whole. This work might be road building or some similar project. Some communal efforts were known as the *mita*.

The Spaniards established these institutions in the new regions they had won in America. Through the *encomienda*, the people in the new Spanish colonies were generally apportioned among the *conquistadores*, a certain number of villages being entrusted to individual members and leaders of the conquering armies. One of the most notable grants went to Hernando Cortes, the conqueror of Mexico, who was raised to the status of a noble, with the title of Marques del Valle, and who received control over 22 towns, 23,000 heads of families, and 25,000 square miles. This holding remained in his family until the Wars of Independence at the beginning of the nineteenth century.

The *mita* was also applied in the Spanish American colonies, though in a perverted way. Indians were mobilized to work for varying periods of time in the mines of gold and silver—one of the great prizes discovered by the *conquistadores*. On a more local level, the *mita* was transformed into forced labor by the Indians for the holders of the *encomienda*. In addition to their usual work on the estates, all adult males were expected to work in rotation for longer or shorter periods on other kinds of jobs—as house servants on the plantation, or in the cities, for example—without payment.

In the beginning, the *encomiendas* were granted only for a specified number of years. However, within a short while they became grants for life, and then, for a small payment to the Crown, they could be inherited. Finally, in the early eighteenth century the system was formally abolished, and the *encomiendas* were converted into outright land grants.

LANDHOLDING IN THE NINETEENTH CENTURY

The large landholding system established during the colonial period was not abolished after political independence was attained by most Latin American countries during the first decades of the nineteenth century. Quite the contrary—it was strongly reinforced.

Two reasons why the system of large landholding (or *latifundia* system) was strengthened during the first century of independence were the abolition of one colonial institution and the marked weakening of another. These were the Crown and the Church.

Throughout the colonial period the Spanish Crown periodically sought to soften the exploitation of the peasantry by the holders of the *encomiendas* and land titles. The king's government issued a long list of decrees and laws designed to limit the tribute wrung from the Indians, protect the peasants from physical violence at the hands of the landholders, and improve the lot of those living on the large landholdings. Although the legislation was largely ignored in America, sometimes it was effective, and when the Crown was removed from the scene after independence, so was its occasional intercession on behalf of the landless peasant who made up the great majority of the population of Spanish America.

The Roman Catholic Church played a dual role in colonial Spanish America. On one hand, it was the great Christianizing influence of the conquest, bringing the Indians, and later the Africans, into the bosom of Catholic Christianity. In this role, it sought to shield the Indians and Negroes from the landlords. It administered hospitals and other charitable enterprises serving the landless workers, and sometimes even provided a modicum of education. The Church was a principal advocate of laws to protect the peasant from exploitation by the landowner.

On the other hand, the Church was itself the largest single landlord in colonial Spanish America. It received extensive grants from the Crown. In addition, many pious folk turned all or part of their estates over to the Church in their wills.

Some historians have estimated that about half of the landed property in Mexico either belonged to the Church or was mortgaged to it by the end of the colonial period. The holdings of the Church were more or less comparable in much of the rest of Spanish America. Furthermore, the Church was exempt from taxes paid to the Crown by lay landlords and legally was even more able than laymen to recruit free labor for the construction of buildings on its various properties.

During the first century of independence in Spanish America, the most important political controversy centered around the position and privileges of the Catholic Church. By and large, the Church lost the struggle. As a result, the large landholdings were generally transferred to individual lay landlords, and the Church's position as an intermediary between the *latifundista*, or large landlord, and the people who worked on the land was destroyed. It could no longer offer even the modest protection it had extended in the colonial period to the Indian or Negro tenant exploited on the large *hacienda*.

Note must be taken of the liberal ideas prevalent among many of the political leaders of the nineteenth century. These liberal military men and politicians generally favored a theory of completely private ownership of the land and all other property. Thus, they opposed not only Church ownership of the land, but also any form of ownership other than by private individuals. This meant they were out of sympathy with the Indian communities—where land was owned in common by the community as a whole, rather than by the individual families. Where liberal believers in the sanctity of individual land ownership came to power, they not only deprived the Church of its large estates, but also dissolved the Indian communities. Then, it was relatively easy for sharp *latifundistas* who owned land near the Indian communities, or for predatory people from the cities, to trick the Indians into selling their land, if it was not seized by outright force.

SLAVERY AND THE CASE OF BRAZIL

Where there were large settled Indian populations of a high level of cultural development, based on fixed agriculture, the system of the *encomienda* was successful in that it made possible a permanent system of agricultural production. However, in certain regions the Indians were hunters or practiced shifting agriculture, and would not accept any form of servitude. They either died in slavery or resisted the encroachment until few of them were left.

Since the Spaniards and Portuguese generally did not come to America in order to do hard work, they forced others to do the manual labor necessary on the new lands. Where the Indians did not submit to servitude, the Spaniards and Portuguese imported slaves from Africa.

In those parts of America where Africans were subservient, the system of chattel slavery was the rule, that is, the workers were the property of their employers. This was true along the coastal

Coffee *fazenda* (estate). Minas Gerais, Brazil. General view.

View of coffee bean drying area.

areas of Mexico and Central America, as well as the northern coast of Pacific South America, in Brazil, and the islands of the Caribbean.

In Brazil, settlement was carried out at first through granting huge tracts of land to favorites of the Portuguese royal court. These *donatorios* in turn gave grants of large areas to other people who soon set about cultivating them. Since the Brazilian Indian generally did not accept slavery but fled into the vast interior, Negro slaves were used virtually from the beginning to cultivate sugar, tobacco, and other products for the ready market in Europe.

Coffee plants.

Thus the large plantation based on African slavery became the pattern in northeastern Brazil, and later in the rest of that country.

The same was true in the Caribbean. The Arawak and Carib Indians either died in slavery or fought to the death to escape it. Their place, too, was largely taken by slaves from Africa, and they, like the Negroes in Brazil, were put to work producing sugar, tobacco, and other products with a strong market in Europe.

THE CONTEMPORARY LARGE LANDHOLDING SYSTEM

The pattern of *latifundia* established in the first decades after the Spanish and Portuguese conquest of America in the sixteenth century has persisted down to the present day in much of Latin America. Most of the cultivated land is held either by those who inherited it from the *conquistadores* or who have in one way or another acquired it from their descendants.

The persistence of the pattern is described in the following quotation:

The reality of the agrarian structure is discomforting for anyone who thinks of economic development. Latifundia still prevails in Latin America. It has been estimated that in 1950 some 1.5 per cent of agricultural enterprises, with an average of more than 1,000 hectares per unit, controlled 65 percent of the agricultural land, while at the opposite extreme, 73 per cent of the units, with an average of not more than 20 hectares, represented only 3.7 percent of the area.*

The situation in some countries has been particularly bad. Thus, before agrarian reform, 1.69 percent of the agricultural units in Venezuela took up 74 percent of the cultivated land; in Guatemala 0.51 percent of the agricultural enterprises owned 41 percent of the area cultivated; in Nicaragua, fewer than 400 proprietors controlled a third of the agricultural area. In Bolivia, before the beginning of agrarian reform in 1952, 6 percent of the agricultural units controlled 92 percent of the land; in Chile, before agrarian reform began in 1964, 1.5 percent of the landholdings comprised 75 percent of the agricultural area.†

The *latifundios* that have come down from the Conquest are organized in many different ways, but there are several predominant ones. In the Andean countries of South America, the Indian peasants are generally tenants or sharecroppers. Characteristically, they are allowed the use of small plots of land; in return they are required to work several days a week on the rest of the

---

*Thomas Caroll, "The Land Reform in Latin America," in Alberto Hirschman, *Latin American Issues,* quoted in Victor Urquidi, *Viabilidid Economica de America Latina* (Mexico: Fondo de Cultura Economica, 1961), p. 86.
†*Ibid.*

landowners' land, and also to provide various kinds of personal service.

The writer learned about this obligation of personal service from a group of peasants near Cochabamba, Bolivia, in 1954, a year or so after they had driven off their landlord in the wake of the 1952 Revolution. They said that sometimes they had been assigned to special projects, and sometimes were used as house servants on the *hacienda* or in the landlord's house in town. One peasant's regular assignment had been to accompany his landlord on nightly sprees on the town, after which the Indian usually had to help his drunken landlord home.

Another peasant cited the saddest case of all. "Sometimes," he said, "he put us to work in the kitchen, alongside the women!" Apparently this was regarded as the ultimate indignity.

In contemporary Guatemala, debt slavery and periodical compulsory labor have been the chief features of the labor system of the *latifundia,* as they were in Mexico before the revolution. In the predominantly Negro areas of Brazil and around the Caribbean, very low wages and total dependence of the farm workers and tenants on the landowner have been the norm.

STAGNANCY OF THE LARGE LANDHOLDING SYSTEM

The traditional large landholding system has seriously hampered the modernization of Latin America. It has hindered economic progress, made for widespread illiteracy and ignorance, and prevented a large proportion of the inhabitants from participating actively in the economic and political life of their countries.

From an economic point of view, the traditional large landholding system has provided meager incentive for progress. The large landowner is usually an absentee; he does not live on his *hacienda* or take an active interest in it. So long as his land provides what he considers an adequate income, he does not much care how it is administered. He tends to spend all or virtually all of his income; there is no point in saving a part to invest in modernizing agricultural production since that would only displace labor which he already receives virtually without payment.

For their part, the tenants on the landlord's holdings have no reason to work harder than he does, or save and invest part of their income to improve the use of the land. Any extra effort—even if possible—would serve merely to increase the return of the landlord, and the tenants would benefit hardly at all.

The effect of all this has been a serious lag in economic development. Most of the tenants on the large landholdings are still engaged in subsistence agriculture, producing just enough to provide themselves with a very low level of food, clothing, and shelter. They are virtually "out of the market," buying in a year at most only a few dollars' worth of goods from the rest of the economy. They are thus not effective as customers in the economy. At the same time, due to inefficient methods on the traditional large landholdings, the land in many of the countries is becoming increasingly unable to produce enough food for the growing populations or the raw materials for expanding industries.

The social effect of the traditional *latifundia* has been the semi-servitude of a large part of the rural population of Latin America. The landlord or his foreman remains the absolute master of those who work on the land. The peasants receive little or no schooling, so that approximately half of the population of Latin America is still unable to read and write. Housing and health conditions in the countryside have remained abysmal. The peasants have shared in few of the benefits of modern civilization.

Those peasants who continue to live under the old *latifundia* system have no real role to play as citizens in their respective countries. In some countries they do not even have the right to vote because they cannot read or write. In most cases the landlords have not allowed them to take part in political parties or other groups active in civic affairs.

In addition to the *latifundia,* there has existed the equally inefficient *minifundia.* This is the small landholding, so tiny that it can provide its owner, at best, with only enough income to provide a bare minimum of food, clothing, and housing. The *minifundistas* have insufficient resources to adopt modern methods of cultivation, enjoy adequate health protection, or be able to send their children to school. Traditionally, the *minifundistas* have received little or no credit or technical assistance. Most agriculturalists who are not employees of the *latifundistas* have been *minifundistas*.

THE MODERN PLANTATION

Before examining the struggle to break up the traditional large landholding system, we should note another kind of large-scale agricultural enterprise which has come into being in recent times and is radically different from the outmoded *latifunda*. This is the modern commercial plantation.

The plantation grows products for the world market, unlike the largely subsistence agriculture of the traditional *latifunda*. It is organized to produce sugar, bananas, coffee, cacao, cotton, wheat, meat, and other products for sale to Western Europe and the United States. Then, too, the plantation represents the investment of very substantial capital and uses modern techniques and machinery. It employs wage labor, and its workers are an important part of the market for their countries' manufactured goods. Frequently, trade unions operate among the workers, negotiating improvements in working and living conditions. The workers' children usually attend school and the workers themselves frequently belong to a political group of some importance. Such large plantations, which began to appear in the last decades of the nineteenth century in response to a growing demand for food and raw materials in Europe and the United States, exist on varying scales in the Latin American countries.

Agrarian reform programs in different countries have differed in their treatment of the large modern plantation. Although all agrarian reform programs aim to break up the traditional *latifundia*, some agrarian reform laws protect the plantation on the ground that it contributes to the progress of the economy.

THE CONTROVERSY OVER AGRARIAN REFORM
IN LATIN AMERICA

The issue of agrarian reform has been a subject of wide and bitter controversy in Latin America ever since the first attempts at it were made during the Mexican Revolution in the first decades of this century. Economic, social, political, and even moral arguments have been used to defend both sides of the question.

Those opposed to land redistribution programs base much of their economic argument on the idea that large landholdings are likely to be more efficient than family farms. They argue that at a time when in the United States, which has the most highly developed agriculture in the world, the trend is toward amalgamation of former family farms into ever larger units, it is not good sense to break up big farms in Latin America into small ones.

The counter argument in economic terms, by those who favor agrarian reform and a class of family farmers, is that the United States and Latin America are not at all similar. They argue that the increased size of the farm in the United States is due to growing capital investment in machines and equipment which requires larger areas in order to be economically employed; whereas, in Latin America, the traditional landowner is engaged in no heavy investment, but relies rather on virtually unpaid labor, and allows large parts of his holdings to lie uncultivated. They add that the sharecroppers, cash renters, or low-paid wage laborers on the Latin American *latifundia* have no incentive to expand output but that the incentive would be theirs once they owned the land individually as small family farmers, or even jointly as members of cooperatives.

Those opposed to agrarian reform argue that the peasantry of Latin America is ignorant, would not know how to use the land if they received it, and would almost certainly produce less than now. They add that the peasantry might deplete the land by not preventing erosion and by other careless practices. Their opponents answer that it is the large landholding system which has kept the peasant ignorant, that the peasant is eager to learn, and that once he has his own land he would have special incentive to learn how to use it better.

Those who oppose agrarian reform are likely to argue that because he is uncultured, the peasant is not prepared to become a full citizen and that a peasant should at least know how to read and write before voting, let alone becoming a landowner. They accuse the advocates of agrarian reform of trying to stir up dissension and even subversion among the peasantry, who they say, are satisfied with their lot until the agitators arrive.

The supporters of land redistribution counter that limiting the political power of the peasantry is not only anti-democratic, but is actually designed to serve the interests of the large landowner, who finds ways around the restrictions if he feels that the peasants will vote his way. They say, too, that real political stability will be much more likely when the rural population consists of farmers who own their own land and are eager to get the largest possible return from it, rather than a population of landless people with only poverty to lose from political turmoil or even rebellion.

Moral questions have also been raised by both sides. These issues have been most hotly debated in recent years within the Roman Catholic Church, to which most Latin Americans belong.

The Catholic moral argument against agrarian reform is probably most forcefully presented in a book *Reforma Agraria: Questão de Consciencia* (Agrarian Reform: Question of Conscience), written by two Brazilian prelates, Bishop of Campos Antonio de Castro Mayer, and Archbishop of Diamantina Geraldo de Proança Sigaud, together with two laymen, Plinio Corrêa de Oliveira and Luis Mendonça de Freitas.

The two Brazilian bishops and their lay co-authors argue that agrarian reform "constitutes a clear violation of the 7th Commandment of the Law of God," and that "Catholic moralists unanimously characterize this action as robbery." The conclusion they draw from this is that not only can no Catholic help in enacting or carrying out a land redistribution program, but no good Catholic can accept land given out under such a program.

However, despite the claims of Bishops Castro Mayer and Proança Sigaud that there is "unanimous" support for their point of view among "Catholic moralists," they actually represent only a small minority of the leaders of the Catholic Church in Latin America. The Catholic moral argument *for* agrarian reform was strongly stated by the *Concluding Document* of the Second General Conference of the Latin American Roman Catholic Bishops held in Medellín, Colombia in August and September, 1968. This document noted "the necessity of a human development of the peasant and indigenous masses [which] would not be viable without carrying out fully an authentic and urgent reform of structures and of agrarian policies." It called for redistribution of landholdings "under detailed conditions which legitimize their occupation and their products . . . for the peasant families."

CONCLUSION

The problem of agrarian reform in Latin America has to be considered in light of how the *latifundia* system originated and has developed since independence. It is important to realize that the issue is still hotly disputed in most of the countries of the region, for it is rife with economic, social, and even moral implications.

2 / Varieties of Agrarian Reform in Latin America

In virtue of the fact that the immense majority of the Mexican villages and citizens are no longer owners of the land on which they walk, are without any power to improve their social condition or to dedicate themselves to industry or agriculture, since the lands, woods and waters are monopolized in the hands of a few; for this reason, the powerful proprietors of these monopolies should be expropriated . . . so that the villages and citizens of Mexico can obtain common lands, colonies or legal landholdings . . . fields for sowing and working, so that there will be a total improvement in the prosperity and well being of all Mexicans.*

THIS QUOTATION IS FROM the first great call for agrarian reform in twentieth century Latin America—the so-called Plan de Ayala issued in 1911 by the Mexican revolutionary peasant leader, Emiliano Zapata, whose name became a symbol for the campaign to satisfy the land hunger throughout the hemisphere.

Ever since the outbreak of the Mexican Revolution, and Zapata's call for agrarian reform, the traditional large landholding system of Latin America has been under severe attack. The Mexican Revolution itself struck the first serious blow against the *latifundia,* redistributing much of the land of that republic. Subsequently, major agrarian reforms were undertaken in Bolivia, Venezuela, and Cuba. During the late 1960's large land redistribution programs were begun in Chile and Peru, while other countries have taken the first steps in that direction. Meanwhile, under the Alliance for Progress, agrarian reform has been transformed from a "subversive" idea into a respectable goal to which all of the nations of the hemisphere are at least formally committed.

In this chapter we shall concentrate principally on four of the

*Emiliano Zapata, "Plan de Ayala," quoted by Victor Alba in *Las Ideas Sociales Contemporaneas en Mexico* (Mexico: Fondo de Cultura Economica, 1960), p. 159.

most far-reaching agrarian reform programs—those of Mexico, Bolivia, Venezuela, and Cuba. We shall also discuss in some detail the other significant national agrarian reform programs. Finally, we shall sketch the influence of the Alliance for Progress on the issue of agrarian reform in the hemisphere.

THE MEXICAN REVOLUTION AND AGRARIAN REFORM

The Mexican Revolution began in 1910 as a purely political revolt against the dictatorship of the aging Porfirio Diaz, who had been in power since 1876. However, after the Revolution's first objectives were attained, the movement spilled over as an agrarian insurrection in which the "peons" sought to redress their age-old grievances. Armies made up largely of peasants and led by men of peasant origin such as Zapata and the famous Pancho Villa, fought civil wars across the length and breadth of the republic. Many old manor houses were burned down by the peons, landlords were murdered or forced to flee, and some peasants seized the land of their former masters.

Emiliano Zapata, who first raised the standard of agrarian reform as a basic goal of the Revolution, was a dedicated and vibrant man. He was of mixed ancestry. Pictures of him by his contemporaries show a man of medium height, with spare features and drooping moustachios, who usually wore the all-white peasant clothing and a large sombrero, with two cartridge belts crisscrossing his chest.

Even before the Revolution, Zapata had emerged as a peasant leader in the state of Morelos, organizing tenant farmers and small landholders to present legal protests against the large farmers' encroachments on their properties. As punishment for these activities, he was dragooned into the army and dispatched to a part of the country far from his home state. Once the Revolution began, Zapata organized the peasants in his native Morelos state to seize control of the government in their region, and to distribute the large landholdings among the tenants, sharecroppers, and peons.

A simple and fervent man, Zapata's program was based on the

earth itself: give the land to the peasants. He fought for this from the time he joined the Revolution in 1910 until his death almost nine years later. His honesty, dedication, and self-sacrifice won him not only the fanatical loyalty of his peasant followers in southern Mexico, but also the respect and support of an influential group of young intellectuals who served as his advisers and edited his proclamations and other public papers. For many years after his death, pictures of Zapata, with his intense, staring eyes, looked down from the walls of peasant huts and government offices.

While Zapata was campaigning for land redistribution, the legal basis for agrarian reform was established in Article 27 of the revolutionary Mexican Constituion of 1917. This provided that "in each State and Territory there shall be fixed the maximum area of land which any one individual or legally organized corporation may own," and went on to state that "the excess of the area thus fixed shall be subdivided by the owner within the period set by laws of the respective locality; and these subdivisions shall be offered for sale on such conditions as the respective governments shall approve, in accordance with the said laws."

Subsequently, when the state legislatures moved too slowly to carry out this provision of the constitution, an amendment was adopted to give the federal government control over the whole process of agrarian reform. Another amendment relieved the new peasant owners from any obligation to pay for the land. The first major federal law on agrarian reform was finally passed in 1922, after the restoration of civil peace in the republic, and in the following decade the process of large-scale land redistribution got under way.

The high point of the Mexican agrarian reform was reached during the administration of President Lázaro Cárdenas, between 1934 and 1940. During his term in office, the government redistributed 16.8 million *hectares* (about 41 million acres) of land, compared with the 7.1 million *hectares* (about 17 million acres) redistributed during the previous twenty years. By the end of the Cárdenas administration, approximately half of the cultivated land of Mexico was in the hands of new owners under agrarian reform.

During the six presidential terms since Lázaro Cárdenas left office, the process of land redistribution has continued in Mexico. Although the pace has varied with the different presidents, all six have moved forward the breaking up of the remaining large traditional estates. President Cárdenas' immediate successor, Manuel Ávila Camacho, distributed 6.6 million *hectares;* Miguel Alemán some 5.4 million *hectares;* President Adolfo Ruíz Martínez' administration 3.5 million *hectares;* and President Adolfo López Mateos gave out nearly 17 million *hectares.* The process was carried forward under President Gustavo Diaz Ordaz, and is being intensified under the present administration of Luis Echevarría Alvarez.

DISTINCTIVE FEATURES OF THE MEXICAN AGRARIAN REFORM

Mexico's agrarian reform is distinctive in several ways. The first, of course, is that it pioneered agrarian reform in Latin America. Another is the special form of grant under which the land was redistributed.

Most of the land given out under the Mexican agrarian reform has been granted to peasant communities known as *ejidos.* These communities, which shall be discussed at greater length in a later chapter, have been free to choose whether to cultivate the land collectively or to distribute it among families that compose the *ejidos.* The great majority have chosen the latter. *Ejido* members with parcels of land have received "use rights": they are free to use the land so long as they remain on it, forfeiting it only if they abandon the land for two years or more. However, they are not free to sell, rent, or mortgage the parcels.

Another feature of Mexico's agrarian reform has been the supplementary programs. Perhaps the least effective of these has been the rural credit program. Ever since the 1920's the Mexican government has combined land redistribution with attempts to give credit to some of the recipients. However, except for a short time during the Cárdenas administration, the credit program has not provided more than a fraction of the peasant owners with the funds needed to cultivate their land adequately. The reasons for the insufficiency of government credit include the high rate of default by peasant debtors, lack of adequate funds, and probably a lack of interest by government leaders who felt that their agrarian reform obligations had been adequately met by mere redistribution of land. Inadequate credit has been a major factor in causing increase in output and income of agrarian reform recipients to lag very considerably behind those of private landholders since World War II.

More successful has been the government's effort to extend the cultivable land through irrigation. This was necessary because of the dryness of the high plateau, where most peasants live, and because of the rapid growth of the population, particularly in the rural areas. Hence, successive governments since the 1920's have carried out large-scale plans to irrigate increasing amounts of arid land, both through building large multi-purpose dams and through digging tens of thousands of small wells. Agrarian reform beneficiaries receive preferences in using water provided by irrigation.

However, relatively little has been done to establish an agricultural extension service which could provide the peasant with the know-how for improved cultivation. Only in the 1960's was a serious beginning made to set up a training program for the members of the *ejidos*. Nevertheless, a massive attempt has been made, particularly since the 1960's, to provide the rural population with at least a primary school education.

Another distinctive feature of the agrarian reform is the fact that the landowners are allowed to keep part of their holdings. As we shall indicate later, the former large landlords, reduced to "medium landowners," have made exceedingly good use of the land they were allowed to retain. Then, too, the old landlords have been compensated for the land taken from them. They have been paid in government bonds, although payment has certainly not been equal to the market value of the land.

To recapitulate, the outstanding characteristics of Mexico's agrarian reform are: (1) the reform has radically altered landholding, with at least half of the land under cultivation now in the hands of the beneficiaries; (2) most land grants have been

made on a community basis to the *ejidos,* although within these
most land has been distributed to individual families; (3) the
landowners have been allowed to keep part of their holdings and
have been compensated for the land taken away; (4) the government has launched programs to expand the amount of cultivable
land through irrigation, to extend credit, and to provide technical
assistance, although only the first of these has really been effective.

THE BOLIVIAN NATIONAL REVOLUTION AND AGRARIAN REFORM

The second major agrarian reform in Latin America was begun
in Bolivia in 1952. On April 9, a revolutionary government, led by
a politcal party called Movimiento Nacionalista Revolucionario
(MNR), came to power committed to carrying out a thoroughgoing redistribution of the country's land.

The plight of the Bolivian peasants was particularly difficult.
Most were Indians who did not speak Spanish and who could not
read or write any language. They worked as sharecroppers on the
land of white or *mestizo* (part white, part Indian) landowners.
In return for working on the landlord's land and for periodical
free personal service for the landowner, the peasants were allowed
the use of small portions of land on which to live and raise crops
and keep a few animals for the support of their families. The
peasants were almost completely out of the market, receiving so
little money income they could buy almost nothing, and they took
no part in politics.

Immediately after coming to power, the MNR government of
President Víctor Paz Estenssoro established a Ministry of Peasant
Affairs. Its functions were to help the peasants organize unions,
cooperatives, and other groups, to register their grievances, help
them negotiate collectively with the landowners, and cooperate
with government officials and political leaders in preparing an
agrarian reform law. This law was finally enacted on August 2,
1953.

According to the law, the small parcels of land worked by the peasants became their property on the day the law appeared. The statute provided that the rest of the estate would be divided among the sharecroppers and other landless peasants as soon as the land was surveyed. Then the peasants would be granted titles to their new holdings. They would not have to pay for the land.

The Bolivian Agrarian Reform Law laid down no such structure as the Mexican *ejido*. The land went to the peasants individually, with the decision whether to cultivate it separately or collectively being left to the peasants themselves. However, the peasants could not sell the land, except to the Agrarian Reform Council, during the first twenty years it was in their possession.

The process of actually granting titles to the peasants has proven to be long and difficult. Although within a decade most of the cultivated land in the high plateau—where most of the Indian peasants live—was effectively in the hands of the ex-sharecroppers, by early 1969 reportedly only about half of the beneficiaries had actually received definitive titles to their holdings. The slowness of the process was due largely to the lack of adequate personnel for the very sizable job of surveying and apportioning the estates. However, since 1953 there has been no effective challenge to the peasants' control of the land in the *altiplano* and each of the many governments since that time has gone forward, with greater or less rapidity, with the process of distributing land titles.

Most Bolivian landlords were not allowed to keep any land. Only those who used "modern methods" and wage labor (instead of sharecroppers) were so entitled under the law, but in practice many of the "modern" farmers were also dispossessed. Nor were most landowners compensated. The law provided for compensation in bonds, but soaring prices in Bolivia after the Revolution made the bonds almost worthless, and most landlords did not even bother to obtain them.

In attempting to carry out the reform, the government soon came up against the heavy weight of the past. A large part of the Indian beneficiaries of redistribution had little experience with—or interest in—a market economy. For almost a decade they were reluctant to increase the agricultural and grazing products brought to market.

The revolutionary governments attempted to change this. One method was the extension of credit through the Agricultural Credit Bank. However, the bank was never able to provide its "supervised credit" for more than a small fraction of the country's new landowners.

More important were the "agricultural extension" efforts of the Bolivian Ministry of Peasant Affairs and the United States Agency for International Development (AID). These two agencies labored long and patiently on a program to interest the highland Indians in sowing more productive seeds for grains, in selective breeding of their sheep and llamas, and even in selling wool and meat. By the late 1960's the program was finally bearing substantial results.

Another change has come about, this time in the contours of the country's politics. The Indian peasants, who came to possess guns as well as land, were transformed by the Revolution and the agrarian reform into a major political force. All administrations after 1952 have rested upon the peasantry as at least one of its main pillars of support.

The Bolivian agrarian reform thus differed from that of Mexico in not prescribing a preconceived form of organization such as the *ejido,* the decision being left to the peasants, most of whom have opted for individual holdings. Also, unlike Mexico, Bolivia deprived most large landholders of all their land; and although compensation was provided for, most former landlords have not in fact received anything. Finally, the Bolivian government's resources have been inadequate to the credit and technical assistance needed by agrarian reform beneficiaries, although some help has come from the United States AID program.

THE VENEZUELAN AGRARIAN REFORM

In Venezuela a major agrarian reform has taken place since 1959 in a broad plan to transform the economy, society, and political life of that republic. Until 1964 no Venezuelan president had turned over his office to a democratically elected successor.

The country had a long and almost unbroken history of military dictatorships. Agrarian reform was part of a general effort to establish an economic and social base for a democratic form of government.

In December, 1958—eleven months after the fall of General Marcos Pérez Jiménez, the last of the military dictators—Rómulo Bétancourt, leader of the Acción Democrática Party, was elected president. During his five-year administration agrarian reform was launched. A comprehensive law was passed early in 1960, providing for government purchase (with payment in bonds and cash) of large estates and the division of the land among the peasants who occupied it, as well as among other landless rural folk.

By the time President Bétancourt left office early in 1964, more than 50,000 peasant families had received land under this program. Five years later, when Bétancourt's successor, Raúl Leoni, left office, almost 160,000 peasants had been settled on about 8.5 million acres of their own land. The process has continued under President Rafael Caldera, who came into office in 1969.

Both private and government land has been redistributed under the Venezuelan agrarian reform program. In the central states of Miranda, Aragua, Carabobo, and Yaracuy most of the land was taken from private owners, because the bulk of the land there was in private hands. However, in some other parts of the country, the government owned most of the land, and some of it was distributed to settle peasants on holdings of their own. By the end of the Leoni administration in 1969 a little less than half of the land on which peasants had been settled had been taken from private owners, the remainder from the national, state, and municipal governments.

Several features have been distinctive to Venezuela's agrarian reform. One is the extensive supplementary expenditures by the government to assure that the land redistribution would be both an economic and social success. A second is the spectacular increase in agricultural output, while agrarian reform was under way, unlike the short-term experience in most other Latin American countries. A third has been the political importance of agrarian reform program in solidifying a stable democracy.

The Venezuelan reformers were privileged in that the abundant financial resources of the government, arising from the oil industry, made possible the investment of unusually large sums in the programs supplementing land redistribution. The Bétancourt and Leoni governments were particularly liberal in extending credit to the new landowners, the great majority of whom benefited from loans from the government's Banco Agricola y Pecuario (Agricultural and Grazing Bank). These administrations also launched a large rural housing program, building almost 75,000 houses for the peasants during the 1959–69 period. Virtually every rural village and hamlet was provided with either running water, a sewage system, a small clinic, or all of these. Schools and teachers were made available for almost all of the rural children of primary school age. Finally, large sums were spent on building local roads to the farmers' markets, as well as on irrigation projects.

The Venezuelan agrarian reform stands out for its very marked increase in agricultural production. Not only did the much-feared decrease not take place, but Venezuela became largely self-sufficient in a number of important commodities while land reform was going forward. This was probably due in large part to the extensive and varied investments of the Venezuelan government, as well as to the increase in cultivated acreage under agrarian reform.

Finally, the land redistribution had important political repercussions. The administration of Presidents Bétancourt and Leoni found their firmest political supporters among the peasants who received land or were convinced that they would soon do so. Although these regimes were confronted by military mutinies from the right and the left and attempts by extreme leftists to provoke a guerrilla war, the peasants resisted the dissidents, sometimes with arms in their hands, and provided the Acción Democrática Party with the bulk of its support at the polls in 1963 and 1968.

AGRARIAN REFORM IN CASTRO CUBA

The Cuban Revolution, led by Fidel Castro, who seized power on January 1, 1959, also undertook a program of major land redistribution. But the Cuban experience has differed in important respects from those in other parts of Latin America, largely because of the Communist direction taken by the Revolution itself.

The first agrarian reform law of the Castro government, issued in May, 1959, provided for expropriating all land in excess of certain limits established in the law. Corporations were deprived entirely of the right to own agricultural land. Those from whom land was seized were to be compensated with twenty-year bonds. The newly established Instituto Nacional de Reforma Agraria (INRA, the National Institute of Agrarian Reform) was to give out the land as individual holdings to tenants, agricultural laborers, and others willing to work it, with each peasant family getting a minimum of 66 acres. INRA was also instructed by the law to encourage various kinds of cooperatives among the beneficiaries.

However, after the Castro government began developing in a Communist direction in 1960, the whole reform program was changed. Only a relatively small number of grants went to individuals, while virtually all of the sugar plantations were reorganized as "cooperative farms," run by INRA through appointed managers. In 1962 these so-called cooperatives were converted into state farms, owned by the government itself. Subsequent laws reduced even further the country's private landholdings, expropriating large numbers of medium and small farms, which had not been affected by the first law. Few, if any, of either the large or middle-sized landowners received any compensation.

The Castroist agrarian reform brought about a much greater administrative centralization in Cuban agriculture, and particularly in the sugar industry, than before the Revolution. Much of the cane-growing in pre-Castro Cuba had been in the hands of almost 40,000 *colonos*, tenants who cultivated plots ranging from only a few acres to thousands of acres. About 90 percent of the sugar produced in Cuba was harvested by the *colonos*, and only

10 percent by the sugar mills from land they administered directly.

Since the late 1930's the Cuban *colonos* had enjoyed extensive legal protection. Laws assured them the right to hold their land so long as they paid their rent; put ceilings on the rents; assured the *colonos* a definite percentage of the return from the sugar crop, and limited the right of the sugar mills to use cane from land they administered directly.

However, the Castro government's agrarian reform eliminated all such distinctions. The cooperative farms (and subsequently the state farms) dealt with all the land on the farm as a single unit, and converted all remaining *colonos* into wage workers.

The Cuban agrarian reform thus brought in the Soviet-type state farm as the characteristic agricultural unit. The peasants, tenant farmers, and agricultural laborers did not get the land, which instead was turned over to the National Institute of Agrarian Reform and its subsidiary cooperative and state farms.

In addition, the peasants retaining small landholdings were also regimented by the government. They were all brought into a national organization supervised by the INRA, which laid down what crops the peasants should grow as well as the prices which they should receive.

The Castro government used its vast control over the land to attempt a radical reconstruction of Cuban agriculture. During the first few years of the regime, its leaders believed that Cuba's dependence on sugar production and export was harmful, and they sought to diversify the island's agricultural output. The amount of land devoted to sugar was deliberately reduced, and large areas were turned over to growing rice, vegetables, and a variety of other crops.

This program of agricultural diversification proved to be a disaster. After some initial successes, the new crops generally did not prove feasible, while sugar output dropped as low as during the Great Depression in the early 1930's. Late in 1963 the decision was made to shift back to concentrating on sugar output. The goal was to reach 10,000,000 tons of sugar by 1970, a figure half again as large as in any previous year. By 1969, however, the crop

was still only about half as large as the target for the following
year. In another try for the 10,000,000 tons, the Castro government mobilized hundreds of thousands and perhaps millions of
city people to work as "volunteers" in the sugar cane harvest. But,
although this 1970 campaign yielded more cane than ever before
in the country's history, it fell about a million and a half tons
behind the 10,000,000 goal.

The return to sugar production involved very heavy expenditures in agriculture. Large amounts were spent on developing a
cane-cutting machine, but this had not proved successful as of
1973. Additional amounts were invested in irrigation projects to
extend cane-growing areas, and in improving and augmenting the
equipment of the nation's sugar mills. At the same time, large
amounts went into rebuilding the cattle industry, severely de-

Close-up of sugar cane.

Worker's house on sugar *finca*.

Sugar refinery.

pleted during the early years of the Revolution, and in trying to develop the production of rice, fruits, and vegetables.

Particularly during the early years, the government also poured money into improving the levels of living of the poorer part of the rural population. Housing, schools, electricity, and medical dispensaries were provided to many thousands of peasants for the first time. But as the general level of the Cuban economy fell in the middle 1960's, these expenditures were severely reduced.

Thus, the Cuban agrarian reform also has its special charactertics. The most striking is that it has been carried out as part of a Communist revolution. All large and most medium and small private landholdings were taken over and organized into state farms, without the owners receiving any compensation. And the Castro government has twice attempted to reorient Cuban agriculture.

AGRARIAN REFORM ELSEWHERE IN LATIN AMERICA

Although the four preceding are the first significant agrarian reform programs undertaken in Latin America, several other countries have initiated land redistribution efforts which are of major importance. In addition, token reforms have been undertaken in many other countries.

Agrarian reform was slow in getting underway in Chile. For nearly two decades after World War II the country's agriculture had fallen behind the growing demands of the cities for food and agricultural raw materials, and it was obvious that one of the principal causes was the traditional system of large landholdings.

The first agrarian reform law was not passed until after the establishment of the Alliance for Progress. The government of President Jorge Alessandri pushed through a mild land reform law in 1963 but it was largely ineffective. A major program to redistribute the land was undertaken only after the electoral victory in 1964 of Eduardo Frei, candidate of the Christian Democratic Party. The law enacted by the Frei administration set a maximum on the size of rural landholdings and provided that whole *fundos* could be taken over by the government for a number of reasons—failure to use the land, using it uneconomically, mistreatment of workers—stated in the law. The landowners were to be compensated adequately, partly in cash but mostly in bonds, for the land they lost.

This law provided for a unique way of handling the land taken over. It was to be organized in *asentamientos* or agricultural settlements, designed to last from three to five years. On these, the peasants who were to become the eventual owners were settled and received extensive training in modern farming methods. At the same time, the government invested large sums in equipping the settlements with improved housing, more modern farm buildings, up-to-date machinery, and other essentials for modern farming.

After the period prescribed for the *asentamiento,* the land was to be distributed among its members. Some of it was to be parceled out as separate family farms, the rest in units to be cultivated cooperatively by the *asentamiento* members. The first land grants were actually made late in 1968, and by the end of President Frei's term in office late in 1970 over 20,000 peasant families received titles to their land.

Under the succeeding administration of President Salvador Allende, dominated by the Socialist and Communist parties, and dedicated to taking the country down "the Chilean road to Socialism," significant changes were made in the agrarian reform program. The rapidity of expropriation of land from the large landowners was greatly increased, so that by the middle of 1972 virtually all land subject to the Frei agrarian reform law had been taken by the government.

Second, the Allende government established a new kind of agrarian reform unit, the Centro de Reforma Agraria (CERA). This was a species of collective farm, in which control was shared by elected representatives of the peasants and officials of the government's Agrarian Reform Corporation. However, there was substantial peasant resistance to the CERAs and in many parts of the country peasant pressure forced the government to continue to organize *asentamientos agrarios.* There was also extensive controversy between many peasant leaders and the government over the proposal to set up a single government firm to own and control all of the nation's vineyards.

As in Chile, agrarian reform in Peru has gone forward in several stages. In 1964, the first agrarian reform law was passed. Patterned somewhat on the Bolivian law of 1953, it provided that the small plots of land that the landlords afforded the Indian peasants for their houses and crops would immediately become the property of the peasants. It also laid down that, over a long period of time, the large estates would be expropriated by the government and turned over to those working on them. But the actual transfer was snail-paced. During the administration of President Fernando Belaúnde Terry (1963–68) under whose government the law was passed, the breaking up of the large estates benefited only some 8,000 families.

An important aspect of this first law was the provision exempting the large "industrial" plantations along the coast. Run along modern lines, they used wage labor, producing sugar, cotton, and other goods for the world market. The Congress believed that it would be more efficient to keep the large enterprises than to break them up as small family farms, and so did not put them under this first law.

In October, 1968, President Belaúnde was overthrown by a coup d'état. The military men who took over enacted a considerably more forceful agrarian reform law, covering the coastal plantations as well as the traditional *haciendas* in the highlands. This new law provided for the reorganization of most of the highland *haciendas* into cooperative farms, and for the partial integration of the traditional Indian communities adjacent to the *haciendas* into the new cooperatives.

The rate of expropriation of the large landholdings rose dramatically under the military government. All of the coastal plantations were taken over, and in 1972 were organized into cooperatives run largely by elected representatives of their workers. A majority of the large landholdings of the southern half of the highlands had also been expropriated by the fifth anniversary of the military coup of October 1968.

Agrarian reform in Colombia is our final example of potentially major importance. The first law in that direction was passed as early as 1936, but it was never put into effect. Not until *la violencia* (the time of violence)—almost ten years of virtual civil war between 1948 and 1957—did agrarian reform become an urgent issue. During those years, bitter fighting was waged between peasant adherents of the Conservative and Liberal parties, and the struggle brought out the depth of the unrest in the countryside. In some isolated areas, Communists seized control and carried out a de facto agrarian reform.

With the return of civil peace and the inauguration of President Alberto Lleras Camargo in 1958, there was wide agreement that agrarian reform was indispensable in avoiding further turmoil in the countryside. A new agrarian reform law was passed in 1961, enabling the government to expropriate land from large proprietors where it was not used or was used inadequately. Under certain circumstances, the government was empowered to expropriate *haciendas* even when these conditions did not apply. The owners were to be compensated partly in cash and partly in government bonds.

After the second law, the pace of land redistribution fluctuated with each succeeding administration. The Lleras Camargo government (1958–1962) took energetic measures to begin redistribution. Under his successor, President Guillermo Leon Valencia, the program slackened. However, the movement to settle the landless peasants on holdings of their own regained momentum with the government of President Carlos Lleras Restrepo (1966–1970), and receded once again under President Misael Pastrana (1970–74).

Almost all Latin American countries have adopted some form of agrarian reform. They include Paraguay, Brazil, Ecuador, Panama, Costa Rica, Honduras, Guatemala, and the Dominican Republic. However, in most cases, the law was so weak and the institutions so poorly financed that agrarian reform amounted to no more than a gesture. For example, although an agrarian reform law was passed in Brazil in 1965, almost no progress in land redistribution has been made in eight years. In Panama in 1967 an official of the

Agrarian Reform Institute said that at the rate at which the land was being redistributed, it would take a century to finish the job.

In Honduras, an agrarian reform law was passed in 1962 by the Liberal Party government of President Ramón Villeda Morales. However, when that regime was overthrown in September, 1963, the agrarian reform was brought to a virtual halt.

In Guatemala, the administration of President Jacobo Arbenz (1951–54) began to carry out a thoroughgoing agrarian reform. However, Arbenz was ousted in a military coup in June, 1954, and the first steps were reversed. Subsequent governments have settled a few thousand landless peasants on government-owned land in more or less remote parts of the republic, but little has been done to expropriate private land, in spite of the existence of a law on the books calling for such action.

In spite of only slight progress in actual agrarian reform (with the exception of that in Mexico, Bolivia, Venezuela, Cuba, Chile, and Peru) the idea of agrarian reform became "respectable" in Latin America during the decade of the 1960's. It was no longer eyed as "subversive," at least officially. In a number of countries, although a thoroughgoing agrarian reform had not yet been launched, legislation for it was already on the books, and all that was required was an administration active enough to get the program underway.

THE ALLIANCE FOR PROGRESS AND AGRARIAN REFORM

One reason why agrarian reform became respectable during the 1960's is the Alliance for Progress. As proclaimed by President John F. Kennedy in 1961, the Alliance was to be a cooperative program among twenty of the twenty-one American republics (Cuba remaining outside by its own choice). It was designed to bring about needed reforms, stimulate more rapid economic development through planning and greatly stepped-up investment both by Latin Americans and outsiders, and lay the basis for extending democratic government throughout the hemisphere. One of the major reforms proposed was, of course, agrarian reform.

President Kennedy, in his speech of March 13, 1961 launching the Alliance, referred several times to the pressing need for change in land distribution. Describing the use to which the funds of the Social Trust Fund of the Inter-American Bank were to be put, he spoke of modifying "the archaic systems of taxation and land tenure." A little later he said: ". . . unless necessary social reforms, including tax reform and agrarian reform are freely undertaken . . . our alliance, our revolution and our dream will have failed."

The Punta del Este Conference, which formally established the Alliance for Progress later in 1961, adopted the "Declaration of the Peoples of America." This document listed several goals toward which the countries pledged to work "during the coming years." One of these was detailed in these terms:

To encourage, in accordance with the characteristics of each country, programs of comprehensive agrarian reform, leading to the effective transformation, where required, of unjust structures of land tenure and use, with a view of replacing *latifundia* and dwarf holdings by an equitable system of property so that, supplemented by timely and adequate credit, technical assistance and improved marketing arrangements, the land will become for the man who works it the basis of his economic stability, the foundation of his increasing welfare, and the guarantee of his freedom and dignity.

This formal commitment to the cause of agrarian reform was of considerable political and psychological importance in the Latin American countries. It discredited those politicians who argued that all programs of land redistribution were Communist-inspired. It gave considerable moral and political impetus to the supporters of agrarian reform, and it probably spurred several countries which otherwise might have stood still to undertake at least a beginning.

SUMMARY AND CONCLUSION

Thus, agrarian reform is a major issue in contemporary Latin American life. Land redistribution programs have brought fundamental economic, social, and political changes in Mexico, Bolivia, Venezuela, Cuba, Chile, and Peru. Table I (page 43) outlines the main features of agrarian reform in the first four countries, as dis-

TABLE I

SUMMARY OF AGRARIAN REFORM IN MEXICO, BOLIVIA, VENEZUELA, AND CUBA

Issues	Mexico	Bolivia	Venezuela	Cuba
ACCOMPANYING CIRCUMSTANCES	After fundamental Revolution	As part of fundamental Revolution	By democratic regime as part of fundamental reform program	As part of Communist Revolution
WHO GOT THE LAND	Those who cultivated it	Those who cultivated it	Those who cultivated it	The State
HOW LAND REDISTRIBUTED	To the *ejidos*	To individual peasants and a few cooperatives	To indivdual peasants and a few cooperatives	Principally to state farms
LANDLORDS COMPENSATED?	Yes, in bonds	In law, but not in fact	Yes, in bonds and cash	No
CREDIT TO LAND RECIPIENTS	Inadequate	Almost nonexistent	Relatively adequate	———
TECHNICAL ASSISTANCE	Inadequate	Very modest	Extensive	Extensive
ECONOMIC EFFECT ON AGRICULTURE	Decline in production at first, followed by large increases in production	Decline in output	Dramatic increase in output	Decline, followed by increases through mobilizing most adults in sugar production
POLITICAL EFFECT	A basis of long-term political stability	Made peasants major political force	Helped establish basis for democratic stability	Contributed to solidifying Communist regime

cussed in this chapter and elaborated in more detail in the chapters to come. Elsewhere in Latin America, some steps (largely symbolic) in the direction of agrarian reform have been taken in several other nations. Finally, through the Alliance for Progress, all of the countries of Latin America are at least formally committed to agrarian reform.

3 / Who Gets Land and How

Three distinct ideologies illumined and guided the struggle for new agrarian institutions:

1. The first had its roots deep in the Mexican soil. The organizational form was the *ejido*, a type of land tenure stemming from the Roman *ager publicus* via medieval Spain. It had features parallel to Aztec communal land ownership, still prevalent when Cortes conquered Mexico. . . .

2. The "men of the North"—Villa, Orozco, Carranza, Obregon and Calles—had lived on the periphery of Indian Mexico . . . "Land and Liberty" to them meant the right of each man to own, in fee simple, a plot of ground. . . .

3. The third program was similar to the subsistence homesteads approach of the early depression years in the United States. It provided that the *ejidos* be reconstituted, but as supplementary to existing *haciendas*. . . .*

As THIS QUOTATION from Clarence Senior's study of the Mexican agrarian reform indicates, two of the key issues in land redistribution are who will receive the land and under what circumstances. (As this passage also shows, there are many alternative courses to take. In addition to those described, there is a fourth, taken by Cuba: transferring ownership from large landholders to the State, with the farm workers staying on as wage laborers for the government rather than for their former private employers.)

How these issues are resolved will depend on several factors. One is whether the agrarian reform is carried out in relative calm and without extensive upheaval. In unsettled or revolutionary conditions, the government may have difficulty in formulating a clear policy—or in carrying it out afterwards.

Another key factor is, of course, the political and economic orientation of agrarian reform. A government committed to Marxism-Leninism will favor state-controlled agriculture. On the other hand, a liberal government, under which both State and private

---

*Clarence Senior, *Land Reform and Democracy* (Gainesville: University of Florida Press, 1958), pp. 24–25.

enterprise have a place, will redistribute on a private and cooperative basis.

A third factor will certainly be the nature of the lands which
are to be distributed under the agrarian reform. Flat land planted
with commercial export crops may be suited to a system of large
private cooperatives. Hilly land, on the contrary, may be farmed
most efficiently by individual small landholders. Technical questions like these are likely to influence the form in which land is
transferred.

POSSIBLE ALTERNATIVES

From a theoretical point of view, there are several alternative
ways in which land can be redistributed. One is to grant land outright to individual peasants or small farmers as their personal
property. In this case the recipient would be entitled to mortgage
or sell the land in his turn, as well as use it and pass it on to his
heirs.

In Latin American countries with experience of agrarian reform,
there has been fear that such a complete and immediate grant of
small landholdings to peasants and agricultural laborers would be
to their own disadvantage. The new landholders, unaccustomed
to owning land, might be tricked out of it by entrepreneurs from
the cities or by neighboring large landowners who held on to their
properties. Therefore, even where land was granted to individual
small landholders, governments have generally curbed the right
to mortgage or sell, at least for a certain number of years.

At the other extreme, in ideological terms, is the government
itself taking control of most of the land seized from large landholders. As we know, this is what happened in Cuba, where the
government set up large state farms on which the workers, formerly employees of a private landowner, are now employees of
the State.

The third possibility is some kind of cooperative ownership.
Under this system, peasants receive land as a group rather than
individually, cultivating it together or as separate family plots.
This system of ownership may be applied to all or part of the land

taken from the former large landholders, and it may involve varying degrees of government control. The cooperative system has
been extensively adopted in Mexico and Chile, and, to a smaller
extent, in Bolivia and Venezuela. In Cuba, most of the land was
first organized into government-controlled cooperatives, but was
then transferred outright to the government.

An associated issue is whether those who receive land under an
agrarian reform should pay for it. The principal argument in favor
of payment is that even if only a nominal amount, it will have a
positive psychological effect. Payment strengthens the peasants'
feeling that the land is actually theirs. Furthermore, with a firm
belief that the land is their own, the peasants will be more inclined
to use it well, make improvements, and generally make it more
productive.

However, the major argument against sale to the peasants is
that they are too impoverished to meet payments. It is argued
that even very low payment is a burden on the new landowner,
whose surplus income should go to improve the land and its pro-

Peasants digging potatoes on Bolivian *altiplano*, land they received during
Bolivian Revolution.

ductivity, and to begin raising the level of living for himself and his family. A subsidiary argument is that the land was taken away from the peasant or his forebears in the first place, and he therefore should not have to pay for what was legally his all along.

The Latin American countries which have carried out agrarian reform programs, or have at least passed legislation, have handled this problem in different ways. But, more have made an outright gift of the land than have required the new owners to pay for it.

In the pages that follow, we shall discuss in more detail the way these issues have been dealt with in the four Latin American countries which were the first to have extensive agrarian reforms —Mexico, Bolivia, Venezuela, and Cuba. We shall also note in summary fashion their treatment in other nations in which land redistribution programs have been begun.

Bolivia is the clearest example of a country that has relied mainly on apportioning land to the peasants as family farms. Venezuela is in more or less the same category. Mexico, on the other hand, has relied mostly on a form of cooperative in its agrarian reform. Finally, Cuba is the unique example in Latin America of predominantly state-owned land.

BOLIVIA

The Bolivian Agrarian Reform Law of August 2, 1953, was issued after a year of careful study by the Agrarian Reform Commission headed by Vice-President Hernán Siles, and it reflects some of the historical circumstances peculiar to Bolivia. In formulating the law, the Agrarian Reform Commission had the advice of several Mexican agrarian reform officials, including the director of the National Agrarian Department and several of his chief assistants. The authors of the Bolivian law sought to avoid some of the mistakes, as they saw them, committed in Mexico, particularly a more or less rigid system of cooperative agriculture.

The fundamental principle of the Bolivian law was that the land would be granted individually to the Indian peasants, and they would then be free to choose whether to cultivate it separately on family farms or on a cooperative basis. The great majority chose to keep the family farm unit of cultivation.

The Bolivian law was based on the system of tenure which prevailed in the country until the 1952 Revolution. Under this system, the large landholders allowed each peasant to use a small plot of land, on which he lived, grew crops for his own support, and perhaps kept an animal or two. In return, the peasant was required to work without pay on the part of the estate which the landowner used for his own purposes and support. The small plots of land used by the peasants were declared theirs by the law of August 2, 1953, as of the day the law went into effect. It also provided that the remainder of the former landowner's holding would be divided among the peasantry as soon as it could be surveyed and equitable distribution carried out.

The law also reflected another historical factor. Over the previous five or six decades, powerful individuals—including at least one president—had seized land belonging to Indian communities, transferring the Indian residents to another part of the country and bringing other Indians in to cultivate the land. The agrarian reform law recognized that the peasants living on the land as of 1953 had priority to a share of the estate, but also recognized that anyone who had been forcibly transferred or was directly descended from someone forcibly removed, also had a right to part of the land, if there was enough of it.

The land recipients under the agrarian reform law did not have to pay, since the principle was accepted that they were getting back what had been seized unjustly from them or from their ancestors. All recipients were supposed to get from the government, a title deed indicating their right to their new property. However, the actual distribution of the deeds has gone much more slowly than was foreseen, as a result of shortages of surveyors to ascertain the exact holdings of various potential claimants. By the twentieth anniversary of the law, it was estimated that only slightly more than 50 percent of the new landowners had received titles. Nevertheless, most of the land in the high plateau area of Bolivia was under the effective control of the Indians soon after the issuance of the agrarian reform law.

The Bolivian peasants generally opted for individual family ownership of the land which they have received under the Agrarian Reform Law of 1953. However, in certain parts of the country the tradition of communal ownership of land, going back to pre-Columbian times, has been preserved even among Indians who were landless for several generations, and the Indians have chosen to use the land collectively. In other cases, Indian communities surviving from the pre-Spanish period have been granted land in common.

The Bolivian Indians generally favored family-sized farms despite the government's effort to encourage the formation of cooperatives. The law provided that these could be established in the following cases:

Land conceded to the argiculturalists who associate as a cooperative to obtain the land. . . .

Lands of small and medium proprietors brought together to constitute the capital of the cooperative.

Lands of peasants favored by the division of *latifundia* and who organize a cooperative society to cultivate it.

Lands belonging to agricultural cooperative societies which have been formed in any other way.

During the first administration of President Víctor Paz Estenssoro (1952–56), who launched the agrarian reform, the Ministry of Peasant Affairs sought to stimulate the peasants to organize cooperatives by offering them a privileged position in importing food and other things which their members wanted. However, in the succeeding administration of President Hernán Siles (1956–1960), when the establishment of a single rate of foreign exchange for the unit of national currency—the boliviano—made such preferential treatment impossible, the impetus toward forming cooperatives diminished. In 1966 the government of President René Barrientos passed a new law designed to encourage peasant cooperatives, but it can claim only limited success.

Although the Bolivian peasants did not generally form cooperatives to cultivate their land, they did establish other kinds of cooperative organizations. They joined together to purchase trucks, for example, to get their products to market. They also formed cooperative credit groups to obtain funds for improved cultivation. Only in a very limited number of cases have they combined their land grants to cultivate them as a group instead of on an individual family basis.

VENEZUELA

In Venezuela there was little desire on the part of the peasants to organize cooperatives. Consequently, Venezuela is another case in which the bulk of the land distributed under agrarian reform was granted in the form of separate family plots. Although the peasants usually joined together to petition the government to expropriate a large landholding, when such action was taken, the grants were not usually made to the community as a whole, but rather to the individual peasants belonging to it.

However, in a few cases the peasants themselves, with government encouragement, did form cooperatives to cultivate the land. In addition, numerous cooperative organizations were set up for the purpose of receiving credit from the government's Banco Agricola y Pecuario (Agricultural and Grazing Bank), and to make use of technical assistance from the Ministry of Agriculture and other government institutions.

One aspect of the Venezuelan agrarian reform has not characterized most of the other Latin American cases. For several decades before the 1960 agrarian reform law was passed, peasants had illegally squatted on land belonging to large landowners or the government. As part of the land redistribution program, the government gave most of these squatters titles to the lands which they were occupying and cultivating. In this way, the squatters' tenure was legalized.

During the first decade of the agrarian reform, the government granted land to over 160,000 peasant families. This was a substantial majority of the peasants who were landless at the beginning of the land redistribution process in 1958. Thus, practically overnight, they became the owners of family-sized farms.

In congressional debate over the agrarian reform law, there was vigorous discussion of the question whether or not the recipients of land under the program should pay for it. Some officials of the peasants' federation were in favor of payment, on the grounds that it would strengthen the peasants' feeling of ownership. However, a majority of the federation leaders disagreed, their position was supported by the ruling Acción Democrática Party, and in the end, the peasants were not required to pay for land.

MEXICO

The Mexican agrarian reform is the oldest in contemporary Latin America. Under it, land was distributed under a unique form of organization. This was, of course, the *ejido*, which has become virtually synonymous with the Mexican agrarian reform.

Under the Mexican system, a group of peasants, living on an estate or on the holdings of several landowners, request the government to grant them the land in question. If the government approves their request, it assumes the ownership of the area in question, and then transfers use-title to the members of the group who have requested the land.

The grant of land to a community of peasants results in the establishment of an *ejido*, a name taken from the community lands of Spanish villages during the Middle Ages. The *ejido* is governed by a kind of council of three peasants elected periodically from the members of the community. These three men constitute the *comisariado ejidal*.

The members of the *ejido* are free to choose how they will administer the land placed in their custody by the Mexican government. A small minority of them have decided to cultivate the land communally, as a kind of cooperative farm, in which each member of the group carries on the daily tasks assigned to him by the *comisariado ejidal*. In such instances, the members of the *ejido* are paid at the end of the year a part of the profits proportionate to the amount of work which they have done during the year.

In the great majority of cases, however, the members of the *ejidos* have decided to divide the land of the group among the families making up the *ejido*. Each family is granted control of a portion of the land, which for many purposes becomes its private property. It has the final decision as to what is grown upon its plot, and it usually negotiates its own credit arrangements with the Banco Ejidal (Ejido Bank) or other lending institution. It receives at the end of the year a proportion of the profits of the *ejido* which conforms to the crops which the family has produced and sold.

However, even where the *ejiditarios* (the members of an *ejido*) decide to divide the land among their various families, they do not have full title to the land involved. They are not legally able to mortgage the land or to sell it. They are permitted to pass it on to their heirs, but these must be members of their immediate family, and their names are listed on the back of the title deed which some of the *ejiditarios* have received.

These title deeds were first issued during the administration of President Manuel Ávila Camacho (1940–46). However, the actual issuing of these documents has been very slow, and this has been one of the principal handicaps to getting the *ejiditarios* to make better use of their holdings. Without the title deeds, many of the *ejiditarios* are uncertain whether their right to the land is solid, and so they have not sought to make the best possible use of the land.

The title deed specifies the exact area of the grant. It certifies the right of the *ejiditario* to use the land indefinitely, and provides that he will lose control of it only if he abandons for more than two years the area which has been granted to him, and then only be a decree signed by the President of the Republic.

The *ejiditarios* have not had to pay for the land. In Mexico, as in Bolivia and Venezuela, the feeling has prevailed that the peasants were regaining land that had been unjustly taken away from their Indian ancestors.

The *ejidos* have been given certain special privileges under Mexican law. One of the most important of these has been the right to the use of water provided for by government irrigation projects. This is particularly important in Mexico, where much of the land is arid or semi-arid and must be irrigated to make it productive. Where the government has established an irrigation project, whether by building a dam or digging wells, the *ejidos* are given preferential right to use the water before the private landowners. Not all the land distributed under the Mexican agrarian reform went to the *ejidos*. Particularly in the last several administrations, the presidents of Mexico have granted sizable areas to individual peasants, so that they could establish their own family-sized farms upon these lands. However, since the 1940's more than half the land under cultivation in Mexico is held by the *ejidos*.

The *ejidos* have been the subject of wide controversy in Mexico, particularly since the early 1950's. Critics of the system point out that the productivity of the *ejidos* has lagged drastically behind that of the private landholdings. Consequently, they recommend granting the individual *ejiditarios* full title to the land they cultivate, since one of the major problems facing Mexico is that of increasing agricultural output.

The supporters of the *ejido* have several arguments. Some, from ideological commitment, believe in principle in the *ejido* form of rural organization. Others, more practically, fear that if the *ejiditarios* were given the right to mortgage or sell, they would soon be cheated out of their holdings by moneylenders or other speculators.

The relatively low productivity of the *ejido* is to be explained by several reasons. One is the uncertainty of tenure felt by some of the *ejiditarios*. They are reluctant to invest their labor and their savings in their holdings, because they are uncertain how long they will hold onto them.

For some *ejiditarios*, the exact opposite has undoubtedly made for low productivity. These peasants are too sure of tenure, taking it for granted, and prefer to spend their time and energies on something other than intensive work on their land.

The author has seen the effects in practice. In one *ejido* he visited, given over to growing corn, there was sharp contrast between one *ejiditario*'s long ribbon of corn land and his neighbor's. In one, the corn was seven feet tall, the irrigation ditches were in very good condition, there were no weeds among the corn. In the other, the corn was no more than five feet high, the irrigation ditches were in a bad way, and the weeds were threatening to choke out the corn. However, because the unproductive farmer was not allowed to sell or otherwise dispose of his property, the other farmer could not buy him out. As a result, the overall productivity of the *ejido* was probably lower than it would have been if each member had had full title to his land.

Another reason for low productivity is the fact that *ejiditarios* have been a poor credit risk, and so have not generally been able to obtain necessary funds. Since the *ejiditarios* cannot mortgage their land, private banks have generally not been willing to lend them funds, and the government's Banco Ejidal has lacked sufficient funds to meet all of their needs. Hence, without adequate credit, the *ejiditarios* have not been able to make the best use of their land, and acquire the imputs necessary to obtaining the greater productivity.

Finally, another factor has hampered the economic success of the *ejido*. In many cases the grants to individual *ejiditarios* have been very small. On some *ejidos* they have amounted to no more than one or two acres. With the passage of time, the tendency has been to subdivide some of these holdings, making them even smaller. In such circumstances, *ejiditarios* although continuing to live on the *ejido*, have often been forced to find work on the holdings of nearby private farmers, or to work in an industry in a nearby city, to supplement the income they derive from their share of the *ejido*.

However, in spite of these problems, the *ejido* remains the characteristic institution of the Mexican agrarian reform. The widespread sentiment for changing over to freehold grants of land, which would permit a farmer to sell or mortgage his land, has proven politically impossible because of the influence in the government of politicians favoring the *ejido*.

Whatever the economic drawbacks of the *ejido* system, it has brought about political and psychological changes in the Mexican countryside. The *ejiditarios* have been organized politically, and since the late 1930's they have been a major component of the government political party, the Partido Revolucionario Institucional.

Psychologically, too, the Mexican agrarian reform and the *ejido* have transformed the peasant from a servant into a citizen. Most *ejiditarios* now feel that their rights have been confirmed by the Revolution. Perhaps this is shown by their refusal to take off their hats when talking with people in authority, looking them straight in the eye instead of lowering their gaze.

CUBA

The Cuban case is the one agrarian reform in Latin America in which a Communist system has been applied. Although this was not originally intended in the agrarian reform law enacted by the Castro regime in May, 1959, it was what was actually put into effect by the National Institute of Agrarian Reform (INRA).

The first agrarian reform law of the Castro regime, based on the Constitution of 1940, was drastic, but not Communist-oriented. It provided for a maximum of 400 *hectares* (about 1000 acres) on landholdings in Cuba, and debarred corporations from owning land. It also provided that landless agricultural workers, or peasants with very small holdings, could receive free of charge up to 66 acres of land taken from large landowners. In addition, they would be permitted to buy an additional 99 acres at specified prices.

The first law seemed to provide that the land would be turned over to individual peasants as their private property, although there were some restrictions placed on their selling the property that they were to receive under the reform. However, the law did authorize the formation of cooperatives by those receiving land under its provisions, and directed the National Institute of Agrarian Reform to encourage their establishment.

From the beginning the INRA favored establishing collective farms, since most of its top officials were ideologically committed to that form of agricultural organization. During the first few months of the new regime of 1959, Castro's followers were divided between supporters of Marxism-Leninism and those who advocated opposing economic, social, and political programs. These two factions were influential in differing sectors of the revolutionary government. INRA was one sector predominantly under the control of Marxist-Leninists, whose model was the Soviet collective farm. Although no specific authorization for such farms appeared in the first agrarian reform law, INRA began establishing them immediately, particularly in the sugar fields. On these farms, the peasants were technically co-owners, but the actual functioning of the farms was under the direction of managers named by the National Institute of Agrarian Reform.

As the result of this law in May, 1959, only a few thousand peasants received individual holdings. Most of the land seized by the government was organized into 600 cooperative farms; and 500 state farms were also organized. By 1961 private agriculture accounted for only 63 percent of Cuba's cultivated land.

However, the 1959 law was not the final step in the Cuban agrarian reform. In 1962 Fidel Castro announced that because of the poor economic showing of the collective farms, they would all be converted into state farms. On these, all workers were to become wage-earning employees of the State. The management was still in the hands of directors appointed by the National Institute of Agrarian Reform.

Later, the Castro government again cut back the amount of land under the control of private owners. Many farmers whose holdings were too small to come under the 1959 law lost land in the second agrarian reform of October, 1963, which set a maximum on private land of 65 *hectares* (about 150 acres). As a result of this second law, 70 percent of the country's cultivated land passed into the hands of the State.

In spite of the relatively small part of Cuban agriculture that remained in their hands, the private landholders have continued to produce a disproportionately large percentage of the island's agricultural output. This is particularly the case with the production of chickens, eggs, and truck-gardening crops.

The socialization of Cuban agriculture came about largely because of the ideological beliefs of the officials in charge of agrarian reform, and after the end of 1959, because of the government itself. From its inception, the National Institute of Agrarian Reform was under the control of Marxist-Leninists, and even before the Castro government took a definite Marxist-Leninist line, the INRA was following policies consistent with that philosophy. When the Castro government as a whole became frankly Marxist-Leninist after March, 1961, the socialization of agriculture was only part of the general policy of converting Cuba into a Marxist-Leninist state.

OTHER AGRARIAN REFORMS

Of all the other countries that have initiated agrarian reform in recent years, none has exactly duplicated the pace-setting programs we have already discussed. However, some have borrowed particular features. For example, the Peruvian Agrarian Reform Law of 1964 provided that the plots of land allowed to the Indians by their landlords would immediately become the Indians' property, as in the case of the Bolivian agrarian reform. Peru's second Agrarian Reform Law of 1969 decreed the seizure of the coastal sugar plantations and their organization into cooperative farms. In this action Peru followed the model of the Castro government's early treatment of the Cuban sugar industry; after a struggle between the government and the sugar workers' unions, the Peruvian sugar cooperatives were finally turned over to boards of directors elected by the workers, in 1972.

Virtually all of the other countries have set restrictions on the right of the recipients of land to resell it, as have Bolivia, Venezuela, and Mexico. However, none has adopted anything comparable to the Mexican *ejido*, although the Chilean law of 1967 did establish the *asentamientos*—cooperatives in which farmers could choose whether to cultivate the land on a family-farm basis or collectively. The Allende government subsequently organized Centros de Reforma Agraria as collective farms in a number of areas.

CONCLUSION

It is clear that the various agrarian reform programs in Latin America have varied widely. Several countries have granted virtually all of the land to individual private holders to cultivate as family farms. In others, there has been a mixed system, with some cooperative agriculture supplementing private holdings. In Mexico, the *ejido* has been the predominant though not exclusive form of landholding for the recipients of land. Finally, in Cuba, the socialization of land has been the pattern.

4 / What Happens to the Former Landlords

Terror swept the countryside. Many landowners were murdered, and others had to flee to the cities to save their lives. Less than a month after the decree had gone into effect the Minister of Agriculture said "at least ninety percent have abandoned their properties." Crops were plundered, houses burned and agricultural machinery wrecked. . . .*

YOU HAVE JUST READ a somewhat exaggerated commentary on another important aspect of agrarian reform—the fate of the landlords dispossessed as a result of land redistribution. Dr. Ostria Gutierrez, an opponent of the Bolivian agrarian reform, obviously feels that the former landlords fared very badly in that country.

The recipients of land under agrarian reform are of course not the only ones affected by such a program. Those dispossessed of their holdings are the other side of the situation. It is therefore necessary to take note of the way in which the former owners have been treated by the various agrarian reform programs put into effect in recent decades in Latin America.

Several issues are involved in this problem. One is whether the owners are to be deprived of all the land, or are to be allowed to keep a part. The economic effects of an agrarian reform are likely to be very much influenced by this factor.

A second issue is whether the ex-landlords are to be compensated (and, if so, how much), or deprived of their holdings without compensation. In the first case, the land is said to be "expropriated," and in the latter "confiscated."

The decision regarding compensation depends at least in part on the ideological orientation of the government. It is also likely to depend upon whether land redistribution takes place in an at-

---

*Alberto Ostria Gutierrez, A People Crucified—The Tragedy of Bolivia (New York: The Prestige Book Co., 1958), p. 170.

mosphere of social upheaval or under more peaceful circumstances.

However, no Latin American country, even if it wanted to compensate the landlords fully, would be able to pay in cash. In the first place, no government would have the financial resources for such a staggering sum. And if it were to issue extra currency in order to make payment, the result would be to stimulate inflation (and probably a drain on the nation's foreign exchange resources), which would harm the national economy.

In discussions of agrarian reform, compensation has been one of the most hotly debated issues. The demand for "immediate payment in cash" has often been used as a stratagem by opponents of agrarian reform, knowing as they do that the government could not possibly make full payment in cash. In some nations, the constitution has had to be amended to eliminate the need for complete compensation in currency.

Where governments have offered compensation, they have usually paid only a relatively small part in cash. The rest has been offered in government bonds, of more or less long-term duration, and usually these bonds cannot be sold before they mature. They usually bear very modest interest, particularly as compared with the very high rates of interest which are generally characteristic of the Latin American countries.

The manner in which these questions of compensation have been handled differs from one country to another. We shall look in some detail at the four main examples—Bolivia, Venezuela, Mexico, and Cuba—and sketch very rapidly what has been done in other countries that have commenced agrarian reforms.

THE BOLIVIAN CASE

In Bolivia there has been a wide gap between what was provided for by the Agrarian Reform Law of August 2, 1953, and what actually occurred in practice. This was largely because the agrarian reform program was carried out in an atmosphere of revolution and in the middle of rampant infiltration, which marked the years following the initiation of agrarian reform.

Since the agrarian reform law was basically aimed against "semi-feudal" landholdings cultivated by Indian share-cropping tenants, it exempted certain large landholdings from its full effects. Owners of large *haciendas* cultivated by "modern" methods (defined as using agricultural machinery and wage labor) were allowed to keep a large part of their land, although maximum limits were put on it.

In actual fact, these provisions were not often respected. Many landowners lost all of their holdings. In some cases, particularly in the Cochabamba region, land was occupied by the peasants even before the Institute of Agrarian Reform could decide whether or not the land should be completely expropriated in accordance with the law. In other instances, the landowner himself abandoned his holdings; in still other cases, the agrarian reform authorities completely disregarded how the land had been cultivated under the old regime and seized the land out of hand.

The Bolivian Agrarian Reform Law also provided that land should be expropriated and not confiscated. Compensation was to be in government bonds, to run for twenty-five years, with 2 percent interest being paid for each of the twenty-five years in which the bonds were outstanding. The bonds could not be sold while they were in effect, although they could be passed on to the former landlord's heirs.

However, these provisions of the law were largely inoperative. Many landlords did not even bother to pick up the bonds because of the inflation which wracked the country between 1952 and 1957. The extent of the rise in prices can be judged by the fact that the exchange value of the unit of currency, the boliviano, fell from about 220 to the dollar in 1952 to more than 15,000 to the dollar at the end of 1956. The value of the bonds offered to the landlords thus fell dramatically during these years. For example, a land owner who received bonds worth a million bolivianos, would find that the dollar value of these bonds had fallen between 1952 and 1957 from $4,545 to only $66. Under these circumstances, one can understand the landlords' refusal to bother with the bonds.

Thus, despite the provisions for compensation in the 1953 agrarian reform law, most of the land taken over—and this means the bulk of the land in the high plateau where the majority of the people live—has remained unpaid for or virtually unpaid for.

The issue of what the former *latifundistas* have done with the land which was left to them has virtually not arisen in Bolivia. In most cases, the large landlords lost all of their land. Where they did not, they have converted from sharecropping to wage labor, and their workers' wages have generally been determined by collective bargaining with the farm workers' unions established soon after the Revolution of April, 1952. The Ministry of Peasant Affairs (established after the Revolution) supervises the negotiations to assure that the workers' interests are protected.

The impact of the agrarian reform has been felt chiefly in the highland and valley areas. In the southeast, although some land was expropriated and peasants settled, there still remain large holdings as well as in the northeast, where great cattle ranches survive in private hands.

THE VENEZUELAN CASE

In Venezuela, the situation of the former landlords differs strikingly from that in Bolivia. Most landholdings exceeding specified maximums (the amount depending on the nature and quality of the land) have been subject to the country's agrarian reform law of 1960. The law also provided that where the maximum was exceeded, the whole *hacienda* would be taken over, and this has generally been applied.

However, the Venezuelan landlords offered little resisance to the expropriation of their land. There are probably several reasons for this. For one, relatively few were of the "traditional" kind, the self-conscious elite that traced their families' holdings back to colonial times and even to the Spanish Conquest in the sixteenth century. A large part of the old landed elite had been destroyed during the continuous civil wars which plagued Venezuela during the nineteenth century, particularly during the so-called Federal War of the 1860's, and the first years of the twentieth century. Ownership of land thus counted for much less as a source of social prestige and political influence than in many other Latin American republics.

Another factor softening the landlords' resistance to giving up their land was the fact that large numbers of them also had more important investments in the urban sector of the economy. They were wealthy owners or part-owners in industry or commerce, and so long as they received what they considered adequate compensation for their land, they were not averse to giving it up.

Finally, and most important, the Venezuelan landlords generally have received very adequate compensation. The law provided for negotiations between the landowner and the National Agrarian Institute (IAN) over the price to be paid for the land. If agreement could not be reached, the issue went to a regular civil law court, empowered to set the value. In the great majority of cases, the landlords have not felt the need to take their claims to court, since the prices paid by the IAN have been satisfactory. Even where the courts did intervene, the prices they set were generally quite ample, and were not challenged by the landlords. Indeed, some critics of the Venezuelan agrarian reform have accused the IAN and the courts of paying too much for the land expropriated.

Payment has been in two forms. Generally about 10 percent was paid to the landlord in cash. The rest was paid in special bonds, good for twenty years, which cannot be sold or transferred to other parties (except by inheritance) during that period. These bonds draw interest.

The ability of the Venezuelan government to offer ample compensation to landlords who lose their holdings is due to its unique economic position in Latin America. Government revenues from the country's mammoth oil industry have made possible the payment of substantial sums in cash. And because of price stability in the country, the bonds which made up most of the compensation were readily accepted by the former landowners, and have remained steady in value.

The agrarian reform has not tampered with the large number of middle-sized *haciendas* in the country. Although a rural labor movement, reestablished after the overthrow of the Pérez Jiménez dictatorship in January, 1958, may have raised wage costs in agriculture, this has not hampered the expansion of private agriculture. The operations of the middle-sized *haciendas* have been adequately financed through the government's Agricultural and Grazing Bank. The already substantial investment in this sector of agriculture has continued to expand, particularly in the grazing areas of western Venezuela.

Agricultural output in general has grown during the process of the agrarian reform. During the first decade of the reform, it grew by about 75 percent. However, it is not clear that the increase in productivity per acre or per man rose in proportion to the rise in total output.

THE MEXICAN "SMALL LANDHOLDERS"

The effect of agrarian reform on the efficiency of the former large landholders has been most dramatic in Mexico. There, private landholding and farming have undergone a metamorphosis. Once largely absentee landowners, who took little interest in how their *haciendas* were run, generally using a system of peonage, the landholders in a large part of the country have become increasingly scientific, modern farmers.

Over the decades of the Mexican agrarian reform, the process of expropriating the land of large landowners became institutionalized. The procedure consisted of groups of landless peasants requesting the National Agrarian Department (DAN) to expropriate a given estate. They could do so on the grounds that the land had once been theirs. Or, if the estate exceeded the maximum set by law or was poorly used, the peasants could simply make the request on the grounds that they needed land and were able to work it. If the DAN considered the request justified, it could decree the expropriation of the land. Between 1931 and 1949 the landlord was unable to contest the decision in court. However, by a new law in 1949 he was authorized to go to court for an injunction against the DAN if he thought that the expropriation was not justified or if he was dissatisfied with the selling price paid on it.

Enforcing this orderly procedure was not always possible. Even in recent years, large landholdings have frequently been occupied by peasant squatters, known popularly as "parachutists," who would then demand that the holdings be turned over to them legally. Recent administrations have usually opposed these unauthorized seizures, but in some cases—generally when the estate was subject to the agrarian reform laws—they have yielded to the demands of the squatters and legalized their possession of the land. Not infrequently, the seizures have been organized by opposition political groups to embarrass the administration in power.

The Mexican large landowner was in most cases allowed to keep a part of his former holding, how large a part depended upon the nature and location of the land. In most areas, it was reduced to several hundred acres from the thousands or tens of thousands of acres formerly owned. Consequently, if the landowner was to make a satisfactory income, it was necessary to learn how to make the best possible use of his farm.

In the early decades of the Mexican agrarian reform, particularly during the Cárdenas administration (1934–1940), many large landowners lost all of their holdings, and in many instances the land was expropriated with doubtful legality. However, then, as later, the landowner was compensated for the land in the form of government bonds.

In 1949 the new land law sought, among other things, to strengthen the position of those owners whose holdings were not subject to expropriation under the agrarian reform law. It provided that landowners could obtain "certificates of ineffectability" for areas of 100 *hectares* (about 247 acres) or less of irrigated land and 200 *hectares* or less of other land, which would supposedly guarantee them against expropriation, thereby shoring up their feeling of secure title to the land. Cattlemen as well as owners of farms producing certain crops, including cotton, bananas, coconuts, grapes, coffee, and sugar cane were given assurances in the new law that they would be legally entitled to even larger areas.

Although land redistribution has gone ahead under all of the presidential administrations since Cárdenas, the onetime *latifundista* has adjusted to his new situation with remarkable success. It is he, for the most part, who is to be credited for the fact that the increase in agricultural output has outstripped the sharp rise in the population during the last several decades. The productivity of his land has grown much more rapidly than that of the *ejiditario*. He has eagerly used new high-yield seeds, and invested extensively in capital equipment for his farm.

One reason for the success of the new private farmer is his ability to obtain much more extensive credit than the *ejiditario*. He has not only received extensive loans from the government's Agricultural Credit Bank, but also has available the resources of the private banking system, which willingly lends him money, since, unlike the *ejiditario*, he can mortgage his holdings.

In many cases, cooperation has developed between the private farmer and the *ejiditario* cultivating land which was taken from him. They have worked together on the building of roads and other projects of mutual benefit. The landlord has frequently given work to members of the *ejidos* whose small plots were not large enough to meet their needs.

THE CUBAN WAY

As a result of Cuba's turn toward Marxism-Leninism, the agrarian reform in that country has aimed at wiping out not only the large private landowner, but private farming as a whole. By 1963 about 70 percent of all land in Cuba, including virtually all of the best land, was in the hands of the State.

No real effort was made to compensate the former landowners. Although the first agrarian reform law in May, 1959, provided for payment in the form of special bonds, the National Institute of Agrarian Reform never distributed them.

Even the small private farms remaining after 1963 were put under the tight control of the government. Professor Carmelo Mesa-Lago describes their situation as follows:

The average size of the private farms that survived has been 13.8 *hectares* [about 34 acres] and they have been integrated within the National Association of Small Farmers (ANAP). This organization is under the supervision of the National Institute of Agrarian Reform (INRA) which, in turn, controls the supplying of seeds, fertilizers, tools and credit to the small farmers. Moreover, INRA plans the type of crops that are to be planted, and controls the system of procurement quotas . . . or forced sale of part of the crop to the state, at prices set below the market prices. The "private farm" has become thus converted to sort of a Soviet *kolkhoz,* the only difference being that it is cultivated individually instead of collectively.*

In 1967 when the Castro government launched what it called the "revolutionary offensive," the scale and freedom of operation of private agriculture was further curtailed. The regime seized an unknown number of small holdings in broad areas around Havana and other large cities, incorporating them in so-called "cordons" of land, which were given over to the collective farming of fruits, vegetables, and other food crops for the urban areas.

Furthermore, the freedom of operation of private farms was reduced yet again later on in the "revolutionary offensive." Professor Mesa-Lago notes that "at the end of the year, ANAP agreed not to sell agricultural surpluses from private farms on the free market but to sell all that was produced to INRA on the basis of the low official prices. The government began to pay salaries to the private farmers and to promote 'collective work brigades,' and 'mutual aid groups' which put into common use manpower and equipment."

Thus, private agriculture has largely been eliminated in Cuba. All large and medium holdings were seized by the State without compensation, and even the remaining small holders, a small percentage of whom became owners of land during the first phase of the agrarian reform, were converted into virtual employees of the government. No landholders, large or otherwise, were compensated for the land taken from them, and large numbers of landowners have fled into exile.

OTHER COUNTRIES

Most of the other agrarian reform laws passed in Latin America have conformed more closely to the Venezuelan model than to

*Carmelo Mesa-Lago, "Evolution of the Efficiency of Socialist Technique and Policies in Solving Structural Problems of the Cuban Economy: 1959–68," unpublished ms.

the others we have discussed. In some aspects, however, they seem closer to the Mexican model.

The Colombian Agrarian Reform Law of 1961 has not as a general rule expropriated all of the landlord's land. Four kinds of property came under the range of the law: uncultivated areas, lands used inadequately, holdings cultivated by means of renters or sharecroppers when the landlord did not actually direct the operation or pay part of the costs, and land voluntarily turned over to the Colombian Institute of Agrarian Reform. Where the land was taken because it was not cultivated properly, the landlord was allowed to keep 200 *hectares* (approximately 500 acres).

The Colombian agrarian reform also provided for compensation, to be determined by a form of arbitration. The amount paid varied according to the kind of land involved, the smallest amount being given for uncultivated land.

Agrarian reform in Colombia has been relatively limited in application and so has not had any notable effect on those landowners who were untouched by it. Colombian agriculture has continued to expand its output at a moderate rate since the agrarian reform went into effect in the early 1960's.

The two basic Peruvian agrarian reform laws, of 1964 and 1969, have differed in their handling of the problem. The first law, passed under President Fernando Belaúnde Terry, exempted the large commercial plantations along the coast, on the grounds that they were cultivated efficiently and were an important part of the country's economy. Maximums were imposed on all other holdings, however, the size depending upon whether the land was irrigated, used natural rainfall, or was used for grazing. Also if the Institute of Agrarian Reform found that a large land holding was not being used at all, the government was authorized to take it all; In addition, land cultivated by "feudal" methods, could be seized in its entirety if the tenants' plots were smaller than three times a "family farm" as defined by the Institute of Agrarian Reform for the area involved.

The 1964 agrarian reform law authorized two forms of compensation. If the value of a property was 200,000 *soles* or less, payment was to be completely in money. If the value was higher, payment was to be partly in money and partly in bonds. Unlike the provisions in most other countries, the bonds were to be negotiable, that is, they could be sold by their owners.

The second agrarian reform passed by the government of General Juan Velasco in July, 1969, differed from the first mainly in providing for the expropriation of the sugar and cotton plantations along the coast. In general, the terms for expropriation were similar to those of the earlier law, with varying maximums put on landholdings and compensation paid largely in bonds.

The new Chilean agrarian reform law passed in 1967 has also limited the holdings of large landowners. Other grounds for expropriation of land were also set forth in the law: failure to use holdings adequately and abuse of the workers employed. In such cases, the large landowner stood to lose all of his *fundo,* as the large estates are called in Chile.

These somewhat ambiguous specifications for expropriation have resulted in many complaints by Chilean landowners. For instance, in 1969 the Sociedad Nacional de Agricultura (National Society of Agriculture) presented a respectful but reproachful memorandum to President Eduardo Frei, that said in part: "The agriculturalist does not have a sure guarantee of security and stability, in spite of the declarations of His Excellency the President of the Republic. How can this security and stability offered by Your Excellency to efficient farmers be expressed in a concrete form?"

The Chilean agrarian reform law provided for compensation to be paid in the form of government bonds rather than cash. This made it necessary to amend the Constitution of 1925, which stipulated immediate payment in cash for property seized by the government. The amount to be paid for land would be determined by the value which the landlord had declared for tax purposes. When the Agrarian Reform Corporation (CORA) moves to expropriate a *fundo,* it serves formal notification on the landowner or his representative and publishes a notice in a local newspaper and the government gazette *Diario Oficial*. Notification includes the assessed value of the property, which CORA is proposing to pay. If the landlord objects to the offer, or to any other aspect of the expropriation decree, he may appeal to special agrarian courts set up by the 1967 law. Appeal from these courts may be made to the Supreme Court of Chile. However, while the issue is being adjudicated in the courts, the CORA is empowered to take effective control of the land in question.

It is still too early to tell what effect the agrarian reform will have on the way the large landlords use the land remaining in their hands. During the first years of the reform, some evidence suggests that landowners extended cultivation to areas that had

Lack of water is a major problem for farming and using land in many parts of Latin America. Here is a dried-up river in western Argentina.

been unused, and put other areas under more intensive cultivation in order to avoid expropriation of the land as "idle" or "badly cultivated." However, little statistically reliable information on this is available. After the coming to power of the government of President Salvador Allende in late 1970, there was a tendency by landlords to invest as little as possible in their properties because of fear of their being seized.

CONCLUSION

Treatment of the landowners in Latin America has varied widely under the various agrarian reform programs. The differences have to do with whether and how the landlords have been compensated, whether they have been permitted to keep part of their former holdings, and, if so, how free they have been to use the land remaining in their possession, and what they have actually done with it.

5 / Economic and Educational Support for Agrarian Reform

Agragrian reform must be seen in focus—and in this technicians and statesmen coincide—as a joint, complex, action. It is not enough just to distribute land, without the elimination of antiquated methods of production, which in Venezuela are the Roman plow, the machete, and what is worse, fire; the mechanical sower [must be replaced] by the tractor; and with this technical and financial help there is at the same time guidance of the peasants by a legion of agronomists, veterinarians, experts in agricultural production; and together with this series of measures there is complementary social action, the fight against miserable housing, against diseases; that is to say, using the terminology of modern military strategy that the Agrarian Reform must be carried out as a global war, a total war.*

Agrarian reform, as we know, is essentially the transfer of land from one group of owners to another. However, as Venezuela's former president Romulo Bétancourt indicates in the quotation above, agrarian reform must involve a good deal more than a mere change in ownership.

If agrarian reform is to be a success—economically, socially, and politically—the new possessors of the land must receive credit, technical assistance, help in marketing their products, expanded education, better housing, and many other services. Many different specialized government agencies are needed to carry land redistribution through and to provide all of the supplementary facilities that must go into the program.

In each Latin American country where agrarian reform has been carried out, special new agencies have been established to preside over it. The previously existing organs of government were not adequate to carry out a revolutionary program like redistributing much of the nation's landed property. However, some of

*Romulo Bétancourt, *Posicion y Doctrina* (Caracas: Editorial Cordillera, 1959), p. 193.

the old governmental departments have also collaborated with the agrarian reform process in their fields of special competence.

There are several fairly well-defined categories into which government agencies dealing with agrarian reform fall. These categories are by function:

1. *Land redistribution.* Special organizations have always been established to carry out this new and complicated task.

2. *Credit for agrarian reform beneficiaries.* New banks have usually been set up for this purpose, but this has not always been the case.

3. *Technical assistance for agrarian reform beneficiaries.* Established organs of the Ministry of Agriculture usually provide this, although other agencies of government, including new ones, frequently take part.

4. *Special organizations.* In several countries, special government units have been established to deal with particular aspects of agrarian reform that do not fit into the first three categories. And some existing government agencies are also adapted to dealing with similar aspects of the land redistribution program.

Sometimes the division of work in agrarian reform is not so clear-cut. Agencies established to perform a particular function are also mobilized to take on another.

In the rest of this chapter, we shall discuss the various institutions established to deal with the many aspects of agrarian reform. As before, we shall pay special attention to Mexico, Bolivia, Venezuela, and Cuba, but we shall also take note of the kinds of government agencies involved in some of the agrarian reform programs of other Latin American countries.

MEXICAN AGRARIAN REFORM INSTITUTIONS

The oldest agrarian reform program of all, Mexico's, has evolved a series of institutions to handle various aspects of land redistribution. The core of the program is the National Agrarian Department (DAN). Its chief duties are to designate land to be expropriated and supervise the division into *ejidos* or into individual farms, as the case may be. The DAN also regulates existing *ejidos*, seeing that they observe the provisions of the country's agrarian code. The DAN also maintains a continuing program of research as an adjunct to the agrarian reform program.

The credit needs of the land redistribution program are handled by two institutions, established during the 1920's. The first is the Banco de Credito Ejidal. Set up first as a series of regional banks to service the recipients of land under redistribution, they were later consolidated into a single bank of national scope.

The Banco Ejidal offers "supervised credit" to the members of some *ejidos*. Under this system, the bank lends money to the *ejiditarios* in accordance with an annual plan of cultivation, granting successive portions of the loan as the plan makes progress. The bank also sells the *ejiditario*'s crop, collects the revenue from it, deducts its own debt, and pays the rest of the sales price to the *ejiditario*.

During the administration of President Cárdenas the *ejido* bank system sought to meet the needs of the majority of the nation's *ejiditarios,* but it has fallen hopelessly behind since that time owing to a shortage of funds. Most *ejiditarios* cannot now draw upon the Banco Ejidal. The insufficiency of government credit remains one of the major problems of the Mexican agrarian reform, since the *ejiditarios* are not able to obtain loans from private banks, which will not lend to farmers who cannot mortgage their property.

Another bank was founded at about the same time as the regional *ejido* banks. This was the Banco Nacional de Credito Agricola, which was designed to serve the needs of the former landlords as well as of other medium and small-sized landowners who were not direct beneficiaries of the agrarian reform.

The Mexican Ministry of Agriculture, which in theory has the task of providing technical assistance to the *ejiditarios* and other farmers, has never been particularly well-equipped for this purpose. However, this form of assistance has been extended by the Banco Ejidal to that small minority of *ejidos* which have actually benefited from its credit facilities.

Even more important as technical assistance has been the agricultural research and related activities carried out in Mexico by the Rockefeller Foundation since World War II. Through its efforts, new and highly productive strains of wheat and corn, especially suitable to Mexico, have been developed. The Rockefeller Foundation has not only developed these new strains, but has also set up some extension services for interesting the Mexican farmers in them. Although the private farmers have been most inclined to take advantage of the Foundation's work, some *ejidos* have too.

Another organization, which though not part of the government has semi-official status, is also an essential part of the Mexican agrarian reform. This is the Confederación Nacional Campesin (CNC, the National Peasants' Confederation) established with the encouragement of the government of President Cárdenas. The *ejidos* were encouraged to become members of the CNC, most did and still remain in the confederation. Essentially a lobby for the *ejidos*, its functions are varied: to prevent seizure of the land of the *ejidos*, to obtain credit from the Banco Ejidal, to get technical assistance, and to work for the continuation of the agrarian reform program. The CNC belongs to the government party, the Partido Revolucionario Institucional, constituting the "peasant sector," one of the party's three principal subdivisions.

The Ministerio de Recursos Hidraulicos (Ministry of Irrigation) is another essential part of the agrarian reform program. It was established as a section of the Ministry of Agriculture in the middle 1920's, when it became obvious that there would not be enough land available to mete out to all peasants wanting it. The program of the agency grew during the next two decades, and in 1946 it was established as a separate ministry by President Miguel Alemán.

The work of the Ministry of Irrigation is of key importance to the Mexican agrarian reform. According to the agrarian code, the *ejidos* have preferential rights to land made arable by irrigation, and so most of this land has been turned over to the beneficiaries of the agrarian reform.

Finally, mention should be made of the Instituto Mexicano de Seguro Social. Although this organization, which administers the nation's social security system, was originally established to serve the wage-earning urban population, its scope was enlarged during the administration of President Adolfo López Mateos (1958–1964) to include the members of the country's *ejidos*. This made Mexico one of the few countries in the world whose peasantry is covered by the national social security system.

BOLIVIAN AGRARIAN REFORM INSTITUTIONS

The basic institution of the Bolivian agrarian reform has been the Servicio Nacional de Reforma Agraria. Its job is to decide which land should be expropriated, and to process appeals by landowners contesting expropriations. Once it is decided that a particular holding is to be expropriated, the agency surveys and divides the estate, selecting the peasants who are to be the beneficiaries of redistribution. It is also responsible for distributing titles to the new landowners.

Two other agencies have also been of considerable importance in the Bolivian agrarian reform. One is the Banco Agricola, an institution established sometime before the agrarian reform, but which has adapted to the job of providing credit for the beneficiaries of the land redistribution program. It has been perhaps the least effective instrument of the agrarian reform process because it lacked both sufficient financial resources and the technical personnel necessary to carry out a program of "supervised credit." Such a program requires experts who can check the progress of the peasants who receive loans from the bank, to see that the money is used for the purposes for which it was granted, as well as to give technical advice and assistance. It is not only the bank that is short of such experts—the likelihood is that there are not enough of them in all of Bolivia.

The most unusual and characteristic instrument of the Bolivian agrarian reform has been the Ministry of Peasant Affairs, which would qualify as one of the "special organizations" mentioned at the beginning of this chapter. The leaders of the 1952 Revolution, headed by the Movimiento Nacionalista Revolucionario, believed there was need for a government branch in which the peasants would have full confidence, which they could look to as "their own," turning to it without hesitation to present their requests and even their demands, and where help would be extended with a minimum of red tape.

The Ministry of Peasant Affairs was designed to be such an institution. It was given control over a wide range of affairs having to do with the peasants. During its first year, the ministry's officials spent much of their time aiding the peasants to organize. Until 1952 the Indian peasants counted for next to nothing in national politics and were practically out of the market economically. The revolutionary government established peasant unions to cooperate in the process of agrarian reform, and pending the redistribution of the land, to enter into collective bargaining with landowners who retained their land. The government also sought to mobilize the political and military support of the peasantry. Thus the Ministry of Peasant Affairs helped to organize —with arms taken from the national army—peasant militia units which we temporarily dissolved soon after the Revolution.

During the fifteen months between the victory of the revolutionary government and the enactment of the agrarian reform law, many other functions were assigned to the Ministry of Peasant Affairs. Rural education came under its jurisdiction. The ministry undertook to provide teachers for the many schools the peasants themselves began building. It also organized programs for upgrading the untrained teachers who made up the majority of those posted to educate the children of the peasants.

Extending health services into the countryside also became the ministry's responsibility as did the fomenting of cooperatives. The only major elements of government relations with the peasantry which did not come within its control were the actual land redistribution process, credit activities, and technical assistance.

When the Ministry of Peasant Affairs was established, its supporters argued that the ministry should work itself out of a job. The hope was that after the agrarian reform was carried out and the situation of the Bolivian peasants sufficiently improved, most of the functions of the ministry could be turned over to other governmental agencies. However, it was not until after the coup d'état by General Alfredo Ovando late in 1969 that the first steps were taken to transfer some of the ministry's functions to other branches of government. The rural education service was returned to the Ministry of Education. However, neither General Ovando nor his two successors made any effort to abolish the Ministry of Peasant Affairs. It remains an important branch of the Bolivian government.

Finally, there are the activities in Bolivia of the United States foreign-aid agencies. From the beginning of the agrarian reform program the Agency for International Development and its predecessors worked with the Bolivian government agencies in various programs of agricultural development, particularly in establishing extension services and experimental farms. During the 1960's it cooperated with the Ministry of Peasant Affairs, the Ministry of Agriculture, and other Bolivian government agencies to encourage the peasants to develop their sheep and llama herds. The organizations set up for this purpose purchased wool from the peasants, as well as facilitated its marketing.

THE VENEZUELAN AGRARIAN REFORM INSTITUTIONS

The basic task of the Instituto Agrario Nacional (IAN) has been the actual process of redistributing the land. However, it has over the years also taken on a number of other activities connected with the agrarian reform.

The IAN decides whether a particular estate is subject to expropriation under the 1960 agrarian reform law, and it conducts negotiations with the landlord over the price to be paid. If no agreement can be reached, the IAN refers the issue to court for settlement.

The Instituto Agrario Nacional also decides who is to receive the land. Ultimately, too, the IAN presents the peasant recipients with the certificates of ownership.

However, the IAN's duties are not confined to carrying expropriation through to completion. The Instituto has also provided technical advice and built local roads to link the peasants with their markets. Sometimes, too, it advises the peasants on where to sell their goods. The IAN has even provided housing for the beneficiaries of agrarian reform.

Several other government agencies have participated in agrarian reform. One of the most important is the Banco Agricola y Pecuario. This is an old bank, originally established to meet the credit needs of large landowners. However, with the launching of the land redistribution program, the bank's resources were substantially enlarged under the administration of President Bétancourt, and the increase used to finance the needs of the agrarian reform beneficiaries.

There was some discontent among the peasant beneficiaries over the fact that their credit needs were being met by the same bank that dealt with the remaining large landowners. Largely as a result of this, a law passed in the middle of 1968 assigned the Banco Agricola y Pecuario to deal exclusively with the new landholders established by the agrarian reform. At the same time, a new bank was created to provide loans to the landowners who had not obtained their holdings through the land redistribution program.

A unique organization which has had great importance to the Venezuelan agrarian reform has been the Malaria Service of the Ministry of Health. Originally established to eradicate the malaria that ravaged much of the country until the early 1940's, the service gained so much good will among the peasants that when the Bétancourt government decided to undertake a program of rural housing requiring the cooperation of large numbers of peasants, the Service was called upon to participate.

In the rural housing program of the Malaria Service, materials and technical help are provided by the Service, and the peasants supply most of the physical labor. By the end of the first ten years of the program, the Malaria Service had built about 67,000 peasant houses.

A number of other government institutions cooperated with the agrarian reform program by providing various of the needs of the peasants who had received land. Thus, the government electricity firm, CADAFE, brought electric power to a large part of the countryside; the Ministry of Agriculture organized a technical-assistance service supplementing that work of the Instituto Agrario Nacional; and the Instituto Nacional de Obras Sanitarias (INOS) provided potable water and sewerage facilities in many localities.

THE CUBAN CASE

By all odds the most powerful agency in the Cuban agrarian reform program is the Instituto Nacional de Reforma Agraria (INRA), set up almost immediately after Castro took power. With the enactment of the first agrarian reform law in May, 1959, the INRA began taking over large private landholdings.

From the start, the INRA was controlled by elements favoring a system of collective agriculture like that in the Soviet Union. As a result, most estates seized were organized as collective farms. Subsequently, in 1962 they were converted into state farms, on which the workers became wage laborers with no claims whatsoever to the land.

From the beginning, the Instituto Nacional de Reforma Agraria was charged with much more than merely taking over the estates. It was provided with funds to finance the activities of the farms under its control. Likewise, it began running the industrial units, such as sugar mills, associated with many of the estates. Also, during the first two years the INRA undertook an extensive program of housing for the workers on the estates, as well as providing them with medical assistance. It also organized "peoples' stores," where the workers did most of their shopping.

By the end of 1960 most of the country's manufacturing firms, both foreign and Cuban-owned, were in the hands of the government. As a result, an Industrial Department of the INRA was organized under the leadership of Ernesto "Che" Guevara to administer the firms. It was not until several years later that an independent Ministry of Industries was established to take over this function. During the period when INRA dominated the manufacturing sector, the Instituto was a virtual state within a state, dominating much of the national economy.

Subsequently, various departments of the INRA were separated from it and established as independent agencies. These included the Petroleum Institute, the Mining Institute, the Fishing Institute, and the Irrigation Agency, controlling their respective sectors of the national economy.

AGRARIAN REFORM INSTITUTIONS IN OTHER COUNTRIES

In other Latin American countries with agrarian reform programs, agencies similar to those described have been established. In Colombia, the chief agent for the agrarian reform is the Instituto Colombiano de Reforma Agraria (INCORA), set up under the Agrarian Reform Law of December 13, 1961. The Instituto has a variety of powers, including the carrying out of a general survey of land ownership, reasserting government control over state land illegally occupied by private individuals, and decreeing the expropriation of other private landholdings coming under the law. It was likewise entitled to decree the distribution of government-owned land to landless peasants.

The agrarian reform law established a Social Agrarian Council to develop general policy for the land redistribution program and oversee the work of INCORA. There also is the Agrarian Credit Bank, an institution of long standing, which extends credit to the beneficiaries of the agrarian reform; while the Ministry of Agriculture provides technical assistance and extension services to the new small landowners.

In Peru, the first agrarian reform law of 1964 established the Instituto de Reforma y Promoción Agraria, the most important organ of the agrarian reform. Its varied tasks included issuing of land titles to the peasants for the plots of land they had worked for their own benefit under the *hacienda* proprietors. It also was empowered to designate various parts of the country as "areas of agrarian reform," and to undertake the actual expropriation of individual *haciendas* before dividing them among the peasants. Other institutions were established to oversee the process of land redistribution and to finance the whole program.

The second Peruvian agrarian reform law, passed by the government of General Juan Velasco in June, 1969, simplified the agrarian reform organizations. The Instituto de Reforma y Pro-

Terraces for farming in the Andes. The Incas developed the art of terracing the mountain sides and the Indians of today continue the same tradition.

Peasants tilling the soil with a foot plow similar to that used by the Incas 500 years ago in the area of Cuzco, Peru.

moción Agraria was incorporated into the Ministry of Agriculture as a new department with a different name, and virtually all of the administrative work of redistributing the land was entrusted to it. In addition, the law created a new agrarian court to resolve any conflicts originating from the application of the law. No special agrarian courts had been established by the earlier law.

An agricultural bank was entrusted with the function that had been carried out by a special corporation under the Belaúnde law. This bank was to issue agrarian reform bonds, as well as pay the interest on them, and receive money from those peasants who had to pay for their new land.

Under the Chilean agrarian reform laws of the 1960's, two main agencies were set up to carry out their provisions. The first was the Corporación de Reforma Agraria (CORA), which decided what estates would be expropriated, assumed title over these properties, and established the value of the land which was being taken. These decisions were all subject to appeal in the courts, although in most instances they were uncontested. The CORA also supervised the "agrarian settlements" set up under the laws and invested sizable quantities of money in them.

The second main agency in Chile was the Instituto Nacional de Desarrollo Agropecuario (INDAP). Its principal concerns have been to aid the country's small farmers, establish various kinds of cooperatives among them, and provide the cooperatives with funds. It also provided these cooperatives with technical assistance and instruction in improved cultivation, as well as helping with the marketing of their products.

No special agrarian reform bank was set up to finance Chile's land redistribution. The major reason for this was the fact that both the CORA and the INDAP had substantial funds available to support the activities of the agrarian settlements and small farmers.

SUMMARY AND CONCLUSION

In all Latin American countries with noteworthy progress in agrarian reform, special agencies were created to direct the actual

TABLE II

AGRARIAN REFORM INSTITUTIONS

Country	Land Distribution	Credit	Technical Assistance	Other Functions
MEXICO	Departamento Agrario Nacional	Banco de Credito Ejidal and Banco Agricola	Ministry of Agriculture and Rockefeller Foundation	Social Security Institute
BOLIVIA	Servicio Nacional de Reforma Agraria	Banco Agricola	Ministry of Agriculture and U.S. AID agency	Ministry of Peasant Affairs
VENEZUELA	Instituto Agrario Nacional	Banco Agricola y Pecuario	Ministry of Agriculture	Malaria Service, INOS, CADAFE
CUBA	Instituto Nacional de Reforma Agraria	Instituto Nacional de Reforma Agraria	Instituto Nacional de Reforma Agraria	———

process. Although all of these are charged primarily with the task of redistributing the land, several have undertaken functions that go far beyond this process. The core agencies of agrarian reform are also supplemented by others with the accessory tasks of extending credit, supplying technical assistance, and giving other aid.

In Table II (page 84) are shown the main agencies involved in agrarian reform in Mexico, Bolivia, Venezuela, and Cuba.

6 / The Organization
of Rural Workers

Whereas, millions of rural workers throughout the American Hemisphere continue to remain impoverished, miserably paid, undernourished, illiterate, plagued by disease, neglected by their governments and still ignorant of their basic rights as citizens;

The VI ORIT [Organizacion Regional Interamericana de Trabajadores] Continental Congress resolves . . . to encourage its own affiliates to increase their rural organizing programs . . . to insist, by every means possible . . . that the land be turned over to those who work it . . . to establish a Rural Workers Section within ORIT's Department of Organization . . . in order that the rural workers may attain the objectives which they share with ORIT: Bread, Peace and Freedom.*

As UNDERSCORED BY THIS resolution of a congress of the largest hemispheric labor organization in the Americas, a close connection exists between the process of agrarian reform and the associations of rural workers and tenants in unions and other organizations. Such associations are not only necessary to facilitate the actual process of land redistribution, they are also essential to bringing about the total transformation of the role of the rural workers in Latin America.

Organizing the agricultural wage earners, tenants, sharecroppers, and other farm workers is of key importance for several reasons. In the first place, it represents the first important change in traditional rural society, actually preparing the way for agrarian reform. Second, it establishes a political base on which to build further economic and social reforms in the agricultural sector. Finally, the farm workers organizations are essential to the process of land redistribution itself.

For centuries the agricultural workers have been the most oppressed segment of Latin American society. Often differing in race

---

*Proceedings of the Sixth Congress of the Inter American Regional Organization of Workers, Mexico, 1965, pp. 102–103.

and sometimes even in language from the landowners, they have been largely silent and unorganized, unable to express themselves except in sporadic violence against the landlords. With the development of rural unionism on a major scale in the last few decades the situation has begun to change.

Rural unions, whether composed of wage earners or tenants and sharecroppers, use collective bargaining as a fundamental part of their activities. Agricultural employee unions negotiate with the employers concerning wages, hours, working conditions, social benefits, and a number of other issues. Organizations of tenants or sharecroppers also bargain with the landlords over the level of money rent payments or the share of their crop which the peasants must pay to the owners of the land.

Collective bargaining has much more than economic importance. Besides the benefits in increased incomes and improved living standards for the workers or tenants, the change in social relations is even more significant. The landlords are compelled to deal with their workers or tenants more or less on terms of equality, rather than on the old basis of master and servant, which has persisted in Latin America since the days of the *conquistadores*. The idea that landlords possessed all power and responsibility, while the workers or tenants were their "natural" dependents, is undermined by the process of collective negotiation between the landowners or their representatives on the one hand and the elected leaders of the peasants and workers on the other.

However, rural unions do much more than engage in collective bargaining. They are usually active in politics. Whether or not they are associated with a particular political party, they promote the interests of their members in the political arena. They may seek legal regulation of the landlord-tenant relationship, or legislation on rural labor-management relations. Sooner or later, these organizations are likely to provide major political backing for a redistribution of the land.

In the agrarian reform process, too, the unions are indispensable. The government land-redistribution agency would find it almost impossible to carry out its tasks without the unions; they bring the peasants together and help decide which families should be apportioned land. No administration could hope to deal individually with all of the peasants on these matters.

In the pages that follow, we shall focus attention on the role of rural unionism in the four countries which first launched significant agrarian reforms—Mexico, Bolivia, Venezuela, and Cuba— and outline briefly the rural labor movements in other parts of Latin America.

THE MEXICAN RURAL LABOR MOVEMENT

During the early years of the Mexican Revolution, there was extensive organizing among the rural population. Mostly, this took the form of recruitment in the various armies of Francisco Madero, Venustiano Carranza, Pancho Villa, and Emiliano Zapata during the long civil war which marked the earliest phase of the Revolution. Most of the armies of this period (1910–1920) were made up largely of peasants.

It was not until peace finally prevailed after 1920 that durable peasant organizations, designed for peaceful purposes, began to be established. Although many of the early unions were set up as locals of the national trade union confederations—the Confederación Regional Obrera Mexicana and the Confederación General de Trabajadores—a large number of them joined to form the National Agrarian League, headed by Ursulo Galván. For several years, the league was controlled by the Communist Party of Mexico, but when pro-Communist elements in it joined an unsuccessful insurrection against the government in 1929, Communist influence among the peasants rapidly declined. During this period of the 1920's collective bargaining between rural unions and the landowners became widespread, and the peasant movement came to constitute one of the most powerful forces behind the agrarian reform just getting under way in those years.

During the administration of President Cárdenas in the late 1930's the great majority of the peasant groups were welded together in a new national confederation with government backing, the Confederación Nacional Campesina (CNC). It became the

Farmers tilling the soil with a mule-drawn plow in the State of Tlaxcala, Mexico. An example of technology more modern than the foot plow, and still widely used in Latin America today.

Farmer sewing seed by hand in the same village in Tlaxcala, Mexico.

principal defender of the rights of those receiving land under the agrarian reform and most of the *ejidos* joined it. The CNC also became an important part of the government political party, the Partido Revolucionario Mexicano (known since 1946 as the Partido Revolucionario Institucional). Some local CNC units were armed by the government, and the Confederación became a key backer of the agrarian reform efforts of President Cárdenas, who redistributed more land than all of his predecessors had.

Since then the Confederación National Campesina has remained the leading peasant organization. It is still a powerful force within the government party, although its influence has declined with growing industrialization and urbanization. The CNC continues to push for the continuation of the land redistribution program.

Since the early days of the Mexican agrarian reform, peasant unions and other organizations have played a key role in the land redistribution program. Organized groups of peasants request the Departamento Agrario Nacional for land, and once formed into *ejidos,* they have joined the CNC or some national trade union confederation. The CNC and its regional subdivisions have supported requests of their *ejido* affiliates for credit from the *ejido* banks. The local peasant groups and the CNC have also resisted attempts by greedy politicians and others to deprive the *ejidos* of their lands.

In the early 1960's some dissatisfaction developed with the functioning of the CNC. As a result, a new peasant group came into being, the Confederación Nacional Campesina Independiente (CNCI), in which the influence of leftwing political groups opposed to the government was substantial. However, within a few years, the CNCI split into two rival groups, using the same name, and the larger of these sought admission to the government party as part of its peasant sector.

THE BOLIVIAN PEASANT MOVEMENT

The Bolivian peasant movement did not assume national importance until after the Bolivian national Revolution of April 9, 1952. Although previously, an anarchist movement had organized a few peasant unions in the vicinity of the capital, La Paz, these unions did not have any importance in national affairs. Generally, the Bolivian Indian peasant was inert, withdrawn, largely outside of the economy of the nation, and completely out of its political life. There were virtually no organizations to present his point of view and represent his interests.

After the Movimiento Nacionalista Revolucionario Party (MNR) took power in the Revolution, the new government established the Ministry of Peasant Affairs, which was intended to be looked on by the peasants as ministering to their needs. During the first year after the Revolution, it was specially concerned with organizing various kinds of groups among the Indian peasants.

Three kinds of groups were set up during this period. One was the peasant union. Pending the redistribution of the land among the peasants, the unions were to negotiate with the landowners, who were required from the day of the Revolution to pay wages to the peasants for the work they performed on land used by the landlords for their own needs.

The second kind of group established among the peasants was the militia unit. During its first years in power, the MNR government, which had dissolved the traditional army, depended principally upon armed units of the peasantry, the mine workers, and the industrial workers in the cities. The small arms that had belonged to the regular army were distributed to the various militia groups, most of them to the peasant units. A third kind of rural organization established in 1952–53 was the local peasant unit of the revolutionary party, the MNR. These party units were sometimes almost indistinguishable from the peasant unions.

The revolutionary government had several reasons for its policy. One was the desire to mobilize political and military support for the new regime. A second was to begin incorporating the Indian peasants into the society and economy of the nation. Finally, the government was undoubtedly anxious to establish organizations with which it could deal during the projected agrarian reform.

Although the militia groups became increasingly inactive with the passage of time, as did the local MNR peasant units, the rural unions remained active. They were brought together on a national basis in a peasants' confederation. The local units of the confederation played a major role in handling peasant requests for land and in working out the details of how the large estates were to be divided among individual peasant families. On those estates which had not yet been taken over, the peasant unions continued to bargain with the employers concerning wages and other conditons of employment.

The political role of the peasant organizations remained a major one after 1952, through various changes of government. After the overthrow of the MNR by the military in November, 1964, the peasants became one of the principal forces backing the government of General René Barrientos, a former MNR leader. This backing was demonstrated clearly in 1967 when Ernesto "Che" Guevara failed completely in his attempt to arouse the peasantry to revolt.

In effect, the peasants were willing to support any government protecting their possession of the land. Thus, when General Alfredo Ovando seized power late in 1969 and pledged his backing for the land redistribution program, most of the peasants shifted their allegiance to him. The same thing happened during the government of General Juan José Torres in 1970–71. With the advent of the administration of Colonel Hugo Banzer, in which for the first time in seven years the MNR shared power, in 1971, peasant organizations became particularly active. The MNR succeeded in reestablishing party units among the peasantry in a large part of the country and the principal peasant union groups came once again under MNR control.

THE VENEZUELAN RURAL LABOR MOVEMENT

As in Bolivia, the establishment of a rural workers movement in Venezuela was a prelude to agrarian reform. The first serious attempt to organize the rural workers took place between 1945 and 1948, when the Acción Democrática Party (AD) was in power for the first time. Some five hundred rural workers' unions were established between October 1945 and November 1948, and these unions were merged as the Federación Campesina.

At the same time, the Acción Democrática government launched the first program to redistribute the land. Holdings seized from corrupt officials of previous administrations were the first to be distributed among the peasants, along with some government-owned plots. However, although a general agrarian reform law was passed in the middle of 1948, the overthrow of the AD government in November, 1948, prevented its application.

The campaign to unionize the farm workers was not resumed until the ouster of the military dictator Marcos Pérez Jiménez in January, 1958. Under the provisional government headed by Admiral Wolfgang Larrazabel, Acción Democrática once again began organizing a national peasant movement. Within a few months, a large proportion of the rural workers—wage earners as well as tenants and squatters—were brought into the Federación Campesina, which was under strong Acción Democrática influence. It became a major component of the reconstituted national labor movement, unified in the Confederación de Trabajadores de Venezuela.

The rural unions entered into collective bargaining with wage-paying employers, where such employers existed. In other cases, the unions negotiated with the landowners concerning rental terms, and in some instances squatters formed crude cooperatives through their unions. With the inauguration of Acción Democrática leader Romulo Bétancourt as president early in 1959, the attention of the peasant unions was directed toward the process of agrarian reform.

Early in 1960 a new agrarian reform law was passed. Under this law, the peasant unions assumed a major role in petitioning for land grants. Once the grants had been made, the unions often took on cooperative functions, administering credit from the government's Agricultural and Grazing Bank, as well as helping with community projects such as building roads and houses and organizing marketing facilities.

From the beginning the rural workers' unions were the bulwark of the Acción Democrática Party. When a sizable part of the urban union support for AD broke away in the late 1960's, the peasants remained loyal, providing a large proportion of the party vote, even in 1968 when the AD lost by 30,000 votes to the Christian Democratic *Copei* Party.

THE CUBAN RURAL WORKERS' UNIONS

In spite of the fact that Cuban agricultural workers were more strongly organized than in most other Latin American countries, the rural organizations of Cuba did not play the key role in the agrarian reform process that similar groups did in the countries we have already discussed. This was due to several factors. First, since the land taken from the large landowners passed to the State, there was no need for cooperation by local peasant groups with the National Institute of Agrarian Reform in deciding which land should be seized and which peasants were to receive it. Second, after 1960 the Castro Revolution took a Communist direction and the Cuban labor movement as a whole was deprived of all autonomy; it was converted into a mechanism for mobilizing the workers behind the government's program to nationalize the economy and as a tool to increase worker productivity.

Since the late 1930's, one of the largest and strongest sectors of the Cuban labor movement had been the Federación Nacional de Trabajadores Azucareros, the national sugar workers' union. Two decades before the Castro Revolution in January, 1959, collective bargaining between the plantation and sugar mill owners and the unions was a well-established process.

In addition, for several decades, a strong organization the Asociación de Colonos de Cuba, had been representing the interests of the tenant farmers, or *colonos*, who produced a large percentage of the country's sugar crop. Two decades before Castro, this organization had obtained strong legislation protecting the rights of the tenants, and it negotiated annually with the sugar workers' union and the sugar mill owners concerning the distribution of the proceeds of the sugar crop.

The tobacco industry was another sector in which the rural workers had been strongly organized for several decades. Finally, during the first months of the Castro regime, a fourth major rural workers' group was established, a general union of agricultural workers from most branches other than sugar and tobacco. It quickly became the largest trade union in Cuba.

When the Castro government began to take the Marxist-Leninist road, the sugar workers' union, the tobacco workers' union and the union of other agricultural workers resisted. However, the sugar workers' leaders finally gave in, while the leaders of the other two unions were removed by the government, to be replaced by other more pliable officials.

The rural unions of Cuba thus played virtually no role in the process of agrarian reform. They did not initiate expropriation, as elsewhere, by formally requesting the land; instead, the local representatives of the National Institute of Agrarian Reform seized virtually all of the large landholdings in the areas under their jurisdiction. Nor was the land in any sense turned over to the unions or their members. Rather, most of it was first organized into government-managed collective farms, which in 1962 were transformed into out-and-out state-owned farms.

With the establishment of a Marxist-Leninist government in Cuba, the nature of the whole trade union movement, including the agricultural unions, was changed. From promoting the interests of their members, the unions were transformed into the instruments to spur productivity. At the same time, the unions had to accept the abolition of bonuses for large-scale production in the sugar industry, and a general lowering of the daily wage of the sugar workers.

RURAL UNIONIZATION ELSEWHERE IN LATIN AMERICA

Of the other Latin American countries in which a serious beginning has been made in agrarian reform, the rural workers' organizations are most important in Chile. There rural unionization and agrarian reform proceeded almost simultaneously. Both were supported by the Christian Democratic government of President Eduardo Frei (1964–1970).

The new rural labor movement brought about substantial changes in the economic and social conditions of the Chilean countryside. Between 1966 and 1968 the agreements negotiated with employers achieved close to a 100 percent increase in real wages for the rural workers covered. By the end of 1969 about 100,000 workers in the Chilean central valley had benefited from the agreements.

The social impact of the rural union movement was even more forceful than the economic effect. Although landowners found it quite difficult to adapt to the new situation, they were compelled to deal with their tenants and laborers on a basis of virtual equality, rather than treat them as backward dependents.

The rural labor movement also had political effects. Since most of the agricultural workers' unions were organized under the sponsorship of the Christian Democrats, the organized peasantry became one of the main bulwarks of that party.

Finally, the new rural unions played an important part in the agrarian reform process. In a number of cases, they initiated demands for the expropriation of particular *fundos* or estates. In other instances, the unions cooperated in setting up the "agrarian settlements" provided for under the agrarian reform legislation.

In Peru, the influence of the rural labor movement has been considerably less than in Chile, despite the fact that the organization of agricultural workers there is almost as old as the general trade union movement. In the early 1930's, in the northern part of the country, the trade unionists of the Aprista Party organized the employees of the sugar plantations and other agricultural workers, while in the southern region of Cuzco and Puno, Communists succeeded in establishing some organizations among Indian peasants in the same period. However, rural labor organization never became widespread in Peru.

When the government of General Juan Velasco decreed the expropriation of the sugar plantations in 1969 as part of its revised agrarian reform program, the sugar workers' unions had certain reservations. They resisted government efforts to dissolve them on the grounds that the unions were no longer necessary since the plantations would be run as worker-owned cooperatives; the government finally yielded to the workers. In 1972 the sugar unions finally were able to bring enough pressure on the government to get it to hold elections of members of sugar cooperative boards of directors by the workers.

One of the difficulties faced by both the governments of President Fernando Belaúnde Terry and President Juan Velasco in undertaking their program for agrarian reform was the lack of a rural labor movement. Although both regimes sought to adapt the traditional Indian community organizations to the purposes of agrarian reform, neither launched a major effort to establish rural unions.

In Colombia, one reason why the agrarian reform process has moved less rapidly than in other Latin American countries is probably the weak organization of rural workers. The two major labor organizations never showed any great interest in unionizing the rural workers. The Confederación de Trabajadores de Colombia, a union under the predominant influence of the Liberal Party, never established a major branch among the agricultural workers. Although its rival, the Unión de Trabajadores de Colombia, established under Jesuit influence, always had a rural affiliate, the Federación Agraria Nacional, it never unionized more than a few thousand workers. As a result, little pressure has been brought by the rural workers to begin breaking up the country's large estates. However, since 1970 a large number of rural workers and peasant unions has begun to be organized in various parts of the country, and has begun to exert increased pressure for more rapid agrarian reform.

Elsewhere in Latin America, rural labor movements have made some advances. In Costa Rica, the banana and sugar workers, in the Dominican Republic the sugar workers, in Honduras and Ecuador the banana workers, and in other countries various kinds of agricultural laborers have been organized into unions. In several of these countries they are contributing to mounting pressure for agrarian reform. Thoughout the region, it is likely that the organization of agricultural workers will precede or accompany any serious attempt to carry out agrarian reform.

CONCLUSION

Organizing rural workers into unions has been a key factor in the process of agrarian reform in Latin America. The unions have played an important part in changing the economic and social structure of the countryside in several Latin American nations. They have also generated considerable political support for the program of land redistribution. Finally, they have been an important mechanism through which the actual transfer of the land has been carried out. Cuba is the only country in which agrarian reform on a large scale has occurred where the rural unions have not carried out these roles.

7 / Results of Agrarian Reform

In short, the land tenure or land reform problem is not confined to the agrarian sector. It affects industrialization, urban growth, political stability, and almost all the elements that are involved in the development process. It is perhaps the most vital issue in Latin America today.[*]

THIS QUOTATION clearly indicates the magnitude of the agrarian reform problem in Latin America. It underscores the fact that land redistribution is an integral part of the whole process of modernization in our neighboring republics. Agrarian reform involves the economy, the politics, the social structure, and even the cultural development of all nations where it takes place.

ECONOMIC IMPORTANCE OF AGRARIAN REFORM

Agrarian reform is crucial to economic development in Latin America. The traditional large landholding system kept a large part of the population out of the market. And because of the system's technological backwardness, agriculture is hard put to keep up with the growing demand for food for the rapidly increasing population of the cities and the demand for raw materials in the expanding manufacturing sector of the economy. Sooner or later, therefore, for industrialization and general economic development to move ahead, land redistribution becomes a necessity.

However, it must be understood that in most Latin American countries, considerable industrialization had already taken place before agrarian reform became an economic necessity. This is due to the strategy of industrialization that was employed.

Generally, these nations have begun industrializing through

---

[*]Joseph R. Thome, "The Process of Land Reform in Latin America," *Wisconsin Law Review*, No. 1, Vol. 1968–69, p. 13.

what is known as "import substitution." They begin with manufacturing firms that turn out products which the nations formerly imported. The markets for these products already exist before the firms are established, and until the factories begin operating, the country's needs are supplied from abroad.

Furthermore, the market for manufactured goods tends to expand by the very process of import substitution. Most of the workers joining the labor force of the new manufacturing enterprises have come from agriculture, where they earned very low incomes—if they were paid in money at all. From subsistence farmers, producing their own food, clothing, and even housing, they become wage earners, buying all of the goods they need, and thus entering the market for domestic manufactures.

As a result of the import substitution strategy, the new industries in Latin America have found their markets ready to hand—in the labor force that the industries themselves created. Thus the backward agricultural sector which keeps much of the population out of the market has not hampered the further expansion of these industries.

Nor has the growth of manufacturing been hindered severely by the insufficient food and raw materials produced by the retrograde agriculture. This is because import substitution "saves" foreign exchange. The foreign currency (dollars, francs, pounds sterling) previously used to import manufactured goods can now be diverted, at least in part, to import the food and raw materials which local agriculture cannot produce.

Thus the strategy of import substitution has meant that progress in industrialization could be made without the interests of the industrialists coming into sharp conflict with those of the traditional landlords. Sooner or later, however, the process of import substitution runs down. In those parts of the economy where it was at all practical, the new import-substitution industries will all have been established. The market will be all filled up. At that point, the process can no longer furnish the "motor force" for further growth in manufacturing and other segments of industry.

When the possibilities of import substitution are exhausted, the problems avoided during the process become pressing. If industry is to continue expanding, new markets must be found. It then becomes necessary to reform the traditional *latifundia* system which keeps a large part of the rural population out of the market.

Also, after import substitution has been exhausted, foreign exchange is no longer "saved," so increased demands for food and raw materials can no longer be filled with purchases from abroad. This is another reason why the industrialists come to favor reform of the traditional large landholding system.

Thus, agrarian reform becomes essential if economic development is to continue. Until the *latifundia* system is reformed, there will be insufficient production of food and raw materials and the markets will not be broad enough to permit industry to expand.

SOCIAL IMPACT OF AGRARIAN REFORM

In many Latin American countries, the process of agrarian reform will virtually reverse four and one-half centuries of history. Ever since the arrival of the Spaniards and Portuguese in America, a struggle has gone on between them and their descendants on the one hand, and the Indians on the other. In other cases, the struggle has been between the Europeans and their descendants, and the Africans who were brought to work on the land once the Indians had been exterminated. In both instances, the Europeans and their descendants were until recently the victors in this struggle.

However, under agrarian reform, the continuing struggle has turned. With the redistribution of land to the peasants that has been going on in one form or another in all of the countries with serious agrarian reforms, except Cuba, the scales have shifted in favor of the aboriginal Indians and the early African slaves.

The traditional large landholding system, deriving from the *encomienda* and the *mita* and the slave plantation of colonial times, barred most of the peasantry from sharing the benefits of modern civilization. The peasants generally lacked formal education, adequate medical care, and adequate housing.

Generally, it was to the advantage of the landlords to hold the peasantry in a state of semi-servitude, dependent upon their masters for virtually all their needs: medical help, financial aid, even religious services. The peasants' standard of living was pegged at the point of bare subsistence, so that all their energy was funneled into their labor. Needless to say, under such a system the peasants could hardly organize a serious challenge to the authority of the landlords. In much of rural Latin America, the peasants' servitude was symbolized by the fact that when speaking to the landlord or his representative, the peasant would have to take off his hat and look at the ground.

The redistribution of the large estates under agrarian reform has begun breaking the landlord's hold over the lives of the peasants. As the peasants come to possess the land they cultivate, they are freed of a centuries-old dependence. Then the reform is directed to training the new small landholders to become farmers, capable of handling their new responsibilities.

CULTURAL EFFECT OF AGRARIAN REFORM

Even cultural life in Latin America has been influenced by the process of agrarian reform. Most of the land recipients are of predominantly Indian or Negro ancestry. As they are integrated into the economic, social, and political life of their countries, they attract the interest of artists and intellectuals. Furthermore, the Indians and Negroes themselves feel freer to express their talents in music, art, and literature.

New themes have appeared in the cultural life of these countries. Indian and Negro influences are favored, rather than despised, as before. And, whereas under the old system, the cultural traditions of the landowning class and the peasantry were completely different—virtually constituting two separate nations—there emerges a tendency toward a unified national culture combining elements from both sources.

POLITICAL IMPORTANCE OF LAND REFORM

Redistributing the large landholdings also has a profound effect on the civic and political life of the Latin American countries.

View of the type of large estate that has dominated so much of Latin American agriculture.

Under the traditional system, the peasantry exercised practically no rights of citizenship. Until recently in a number of countries, they were prohibited from participating in elections, either as voters or candidates, because they were illiterate. Since they were unrepresented by their own organizations, they were unable to bring other influence to bear upon the political system. They could not lobby for legislation or other action on their behalf, they were prohibited from engaging in strikes or other protests. Nor did they usually belong to the country's political parties.

All of this changes with agrarian reform, under which the various peasant organizations become an integral part of the process. After the land is redistributed, the organizations continue acting as spokesmen for the new peasant landholders.

Even where literacy was still required in order to vote or hold office after agrarian reform, the extension of education which usually accompanies it has spread literacy among the peasants. More thus qualify for full citizenship.

Another important political change follows in the wake of agrarian reform. Under the traditional large landholding system, if the peasants were allowed to engage in political activity at all, it was only because they could be counted on to support the interests of the landholders. With agrarian reform, they have come to participate in politics in defense of their own interests rather than of those of someone else.

This change has been very great in those countries where agrarian reform has gone farthest. In Bolivia, the peasants emerged as one of the two major power factors in the country's politics—the other being the armed forces. In Mexico, the peasants' principal organization, the Confederación Nacional Campesina, has for more than thirty years been one of the three major components of the government political party, the Partido Revolucionario Institucional. In Venezuela, since 1959, the peasants have constituted the largest and most reliable element supporting the Acción Democrática Party. Even in Chile, the peasants organized in rural unions, and with the prospect of receiving land under the Christian Democratic Party government's agrarian reform program, they were a major center of support for that party. They continued to be so even after the Christian Democratic government had been succeeded by the Marxist one of President Salvador Allende.

Another aspect of the political effects of agrarian reform is the spread of nationalism to segments of the population for whom it had little or no meaning before. In the earlier period, neither the landholding upper class nor the great mass of the peasantry was very nationalistic. The upper class was inclined to be "internationalist" in outlook. They copied models from abroad, whether in cultural affairs, styles of dress and social behavior, or in politics. They felt much closer to their fellow aristocrats in other Latin American countries, or with the upper and middle classes in Europe and the United States than to their own countrymen of the lower class.

On the other hand, the outlook of the peasantry tended to be "parochial." They knew little about anything beyond the *hacienda* on which they lived, or the Indian community to which they belonged. Sometimes they were even ignorant of the existence of the nation of which they were supposed to be a part.

The author encountered a case of this parochialism in Bolivia during the early years of the agrarian reform in that country. A Mexican friend, who did not know the country very well, worked for the Agrarian Reform Service and as part of his work would meet with groups of Indians who came to the Service requesting land. He would refer to a large map behind his desk to find out just where the Indians came from. Not infrequently, he discovered that they lived in Peru. They had no concept of the fact that an international boundary separated them from the country in which land was being distributed to the peasantry.

However, with the advent of the agrarian reform the peasants' outlook has changed. The national government makes its presence felt through concrete acts, in which the peasants participate. Once they feel that they belong, the peasants are actually drawn to the ideology of nationalism. They develop strong feelings of loyalty to the nation; and politicians, knowing this, appeal to them on that basis. As education is extended to the peasantry in the wake of agrarian reform, the peasants learn about the country's history, its symbols, and heroes. Thus, the appeal to the national interest that is an inherent part of nationalism becomes meaningful to them in a way that was impossible under the old system, where loyalties were limited to the local community.

The ideology of nationalism itself changes under the impact of agrarian reform. The good of the nation is reinterpreted to mean the good of all, the peasantry as well as the urban workers, the lower class as well as the upper class—insofar as the latter's interest can be reconciled with that of the nation as a whole. Nationalism in Latin America thus takes on a new and progressive meaning, not really understood in the United States, where nationalism is identified with reaction.

Obviously, the redistribution of land also has a major impact on the distribution of political power. Parties representing the interests of the landowners lose their influence while parties carrying out agrarian reform or supporting it, tend to become dominant.

Agrarian reform thus enhances the possibilities for genuine political democracy. Before agrarian reform, democracy was almost impssible in Latin America. Most of the population did not participate in the political process. Parties and politicians that appealed to the peasants were regarded as "subversive" and harassed by the government, so that most political leaders carefully avoided the issue. However, all this changes once the peasants acquire the land. More and more, the rural people are becoming an integral part of the body politic, and political leaders can ignore them only at their own peril.

THE CUBAN ANOMALY

Cuba does not fit the general pattern of agrarian reform elsewhere in Latin America. Unlike the cases of Bolivia, Venezuela, and even Mexico, the peasants have little or no control over how the land is used. What is planted, how it is grown, and what the selling price will be are all determined by the government, the peasants having very little to say in these matters.

The socialization of agriculture in Cuba has led to many problems that are different from those facing the other agrarian reform programs in Latin America. Agriculture has been the weakest sector of the economies of all other Communist-controlled countries. So far, Cuba has not proved to be an exception.

In trying to make a success of socialized agriculture, the Castro government has faced serious handicaps. On his way to power, Fidel Castro had promised the tenants, sharecroppers, and agricultural laborers of Cuba that after the Revolution they would become owners of their own land. It is doubtful whether the rural people of Cuba are satisfied that the promise has been fulfilled. There is considerable evidence that there has been widespread passive resistance by at least some of the rural population.

The Castro regime's justification for socialized agriculture is largely ideological. Socialization was designed to put the farmers on essentially the same basis as workers in industry or commerce: wage earners employed by the State, which in theory was a "workers' state." The regime has argued that the state farms, like the factories and large industries, belong to "all the workers," and that the nation is advancing toward the ideal "classless society."

In spite of these differences with the other Latin American countries, Cuba has been faced with the same problem of supplementing agrarian reform with agricultural reform. The Castro regime has invested very heavily in capital equipment, irrigation, and other inputs in an effort to raise the technological level of Cuban agriculture. Only Venezuela approaches Cuba in the volume of such investment.

The political impact of agrarian reform in Cuba naturally has no analogue elsewhere in Latin America. The Cuban Revolution led to a dictatorship controlled by the Communist Party, so agrarian reform has not promoted the possibility of political democracy. It should be noted, however, that large numbers of agricultural workers have been brought into the new Communist Party organized after 1961.

INTERNATIONAL IMPACT OF LATIN AMERICAN AGRARIAN REFORM

As we have indicated throughout this book, agrarian reform is part of a broader movement of revolutionary change in Latin America. Land redistribution is advocated not only by democratic supporters of this broader revolution, who are more or less well disposed toward the United States, but also by Marxist-Leninists of various kinds who are violent opponents of the United States.

These facts help to explain the somewhat equivocal attitude of the United States toward agrarian reform. Although extensive help was given to the Bolivian agrarian reform during the 1950's, the United States did not during that period take an official position in favor of the idea as a general policy in Latin America.

It was not until the Kennedy administration that the United States government officially declared its support of agrarian reform. Land redistribution became a fundamental part of the Alliance for Progress, first announced by President Kennedy in April, 1961, and officially adopted by twenty American republics, including the United States, in August of that year. However, after the assassination of President Kennedy, United States support for agrarian reform began to diminish. The government's attitude seemed particularly equivocal after American military intervention in the Dominican Republic in 1965 against a revolution aiming to restore the democratic regime of ex-President Juan Bosch, which had begun a land redistribution program before being overthrown by the military. With the announcement by President Richard Nixon late in 1969 of a new United States policy toward Latin America, which in effect proclaimed social reform in Latin America to be of no concern to this country, American policy came full circle, back to the position it held in the 1950's.

VARIETIES OF AGRARIAN REFORM

Thus the process of land redistribution or agrarian reform, where carried out effectively, marks a turning point in the history of Latin America. So far, only six countries, Mexico, Bolivia, Venezuela, Cuba, Chile and Peru, have actually carried agrarian reform far enough to bring about a fundamental change in the economy and society. Only one other, Colombia, has made appreciable beginnings although virtually all countries in the area have formally enacted land redistribution laws.

The four countries with which we have dealt primarily have each evolved their own way of dealing with the problems confronting them. These varying approaches may be recapitulated as follows:

In Mexico, all large landholdings over certain limits are subject to expropriation, although the landlords are usually allowed to keep a part of their estates and they are compensated in bonds for the acreage they lose. The government grants use-rights but not full title to peasant communities, the *ejidos*, which usually subdivide the land among their members, who are supposed to (but who do not always) receive title deeds to their new property. Credit facilities for the *ejiditarios* have been inadequate, and so has technical assistance. But the government has invested heavily in irrigation to make more land available to the *ejiditarios*, as well as in rural education, and it has extended the social security law to include the *ejido* members. Finally, since 1936 most agrarian

reform beneficiaries have belonged to the national peasants' confederation, one of the three "sectors" of the official government
party, and since at least a decade before that, peasant organizations have played a key role in initiating the process of expropriation.

In Bolivia, virtually all landholdings in the high plateau and in
the major valleys were turned over to the peasants, although by
1973 only a bit more than half of the peasants had actually received title deeds. These deeds restrict the right of the peasants
to mortgage or sell their land for twenty years. Although the law
formally provided for compensation in bonds, rampant inflation
following the reform reduced the bonds' value to a pittance, and
hardly any landlords have claimed them. Rural credit and technical assistance have generally been very inadequate, although in
the 1960's a joint Bolivian–United States program began to make
some headway, and many schools have been built in rural areas.
The land was granted to the peasants on an individual family
basis, and only a small minority chose to cultivate their new holdings on a cooperative basis. The agrarian reform was followed by
a decline in agricultural output during the first few years, but by
the late 1960's this had begun to change. Agrarian reform and the
rise of rural unionism have transformed the peasantry into one of
the major forces in national politics.

In Venezuela, over 160,000 peasant families have received land
on an individual farm basis. Numerous cooperatives have been
created to handle specific problems of purchasing, marketing,
credit, and the like. Land grants limit the right to sell or mortgage
the land for twenty years. Just short of half the land granted was
expropriated from private holders, the remainder being government land. Generally, entire estates have been expropriated, with
the ex-landlords receiving ample compensation, principally in government bonds. Very extensive credit and technical assistance
were provided to the peasant beneficiaries, and the government
also supplied practically all of them with such essential services
as schools, medical dispensaries, electricity, water supplies, and
sewerage facilities. The agrarian reform has been accompanied by
a very large increase in agricultural output. The peasants' federa-

TABLE III

Summary of Major Latin American Agrarian Reforms

	Mexico	Bolivia	Venezuela	Cuba
DATE BEGUN	1915	1952	Originally in 1945–48, renewed in 1958	1959
NUMBER OF PEASANTS AFFECTED	Majority of peasant population	Virtually all those in the heavily populated high plateau	160,000	——
AREA AFFECTED (ACRES)	Over 140 million	Virtually all of high plateau, sizable region in low lands	9 million acres	Virtually all arable land in island
MAJOR CHARACTERISTICS	*Ejido;* growth of production on private farms; peasant participation in government party	Beginning of integration of Indians in society; peasants become important political factor	Intensive government aid to agrarian reform beneficiaries; large growth of output; major role of peasants in AD party	Almost complete socialization of agriculture; government concentration on agriculture, particularly sugar, after 1964
MAJOR AGRARIAN REFORM AGENCY	Departamento Agrario Nacional	Servicio Nacional de Reforma Agraria	Instituto Agrario Nacional	Instituto Nacional de Reforma Agraria
MAJOR AGRICULTURAL WORKERS' GROUPS	Confederación Nacional Campesina	Confederación Campesina	Federación Campesina	Federación Nacional de Trabajadores Azucareros, Federación Tabacalera, Federación Agricolas de Trabajadores

110

tion has played a major role in national politics, constituting the mainstay of the Acción Democrática Party, which was in power from 1959 to 1969, while most of the agrarian reform was being carried out.

The Cuban agrarian reform confiscated all holdings of 66 acres or more, and many farms below that limit. Most of the cultivated land was transferred to the State, which organized it first into collective farms, and later state farms. The former landlords received no compensation. The government has put large sums into agriculture, and during the first few years, into housing, schools, and medical facilities; and subsequently into irrigation, acquisition of capital equipment, road construction, etc. Government planning in agriculture first aimed to diversify production at the expense of sugar during the first few years, and intense concentration on sugar production after 1963. The rural workers' organizations, including the unions of wage earners and the new association of the remaining small holders, are completely subordinate to the government and the Communist Party. Their principal function is to increase workers' productivity and output.

CONCLUSION

Table III (p. 110) shows some of the outstanding characteristics of the agrarian reform in Mexico, Bolivia, Venezuela, and Cuba.

These are some of the ways used to handle the problems arising in the course of carrying out agrarian reform. Those countries which have not yet carried out agrarian reforms will discover when they do, as have the countries preceding them, that agrarian reform is a revolutionary act. It is an essential part of the process of "modernization," transforming a hierarchical, rigidly stratified society with a relatively unproductive agricultural economy into a much more socially mobile, economically diversified, more wealthy, and hopefully, more democratic, society.

Index

Index